SQL Server Interview
Questions, Answers, and
Explanations

By Terry Clark

SQL Interview Questions, Answers, and Explanations

ISBN-13 978-1-933804-77-4
ISBN 1-933804-77-7

By Terry Clark
Edited by Emilee Newman Bowles

Printed in the United States of America

Please visit our website at www.itcookbook.com

Table of Contents

Introduction

SQL Server is a relational database management system (RDBMS) produced by Microsoft. Its primary query language is Transact-SQL, an implementation of the ANSI/ISO standard Structured Query Language (SQL) used by both Microsoft and Sybase. SQL Server is commonly used by businesses for small- to medium-sized databases, but the past five years have seen greater adoption of the product for larger enterprise databases.

History

The code base for Microsoft SQL Server (prior to version 7.0) originated in Sybase SQL Server, and was Microsoft's entry to the enterprise-level database market, competing against Oracle, IBM, and, later, Sybase itself.

Microsoft, Sybase and Ashton-Tate originally teamed up to create and market the first version named SQL Server 1.0 for OS/2 (about 1989) which was essentially the same as Sybase SQL Server 3.0 on Unix, VMS, etc. Microsoft SQL Server 4.2 was shipped around 1992 (available bundled with Microsoft OS/2 version 1.3). Later Microsoft SQL Server 4.21 for Windows NT was released at the same time as Windows NT 3.1. Microsoft SQL Server v6.0 was the first version of SQL Server that was architected for NT and did not include any direction from Sybase.

About the time Windows NT was coming out, however, Sybase and Microsoft parted ways and pursued their own design and marketing schemes. Microsoft negotiated exclusive rights to all versions of SQL Server written for Microsoft operating systems. Later, Sybase changed the name of its product to Adaptive Server Enterprise to avoid confusion with Microsoft SQL Server. Until 1994, Microsoft's SQL Server carried three Sybase copyright notices as an indication of its origin.

Since parting ways, several revisions have been done independently. SQL Server 7.0 was the first true GUI based database server and was a rewrite away from the legacy Sybase code. A variant of SQL Server 2000 was the first commercial database for the Intel IA64 architecture. During this time there was a rivalry between Microsoft and Oracle to win over the enterprise market.

The current version, Microsoft SQL Server 2005, was released in November 2005. The launch took place alongside Visual Studio 2005. The SQL Server 2005 Express Edition is currently available for free download. The Microsoft SQL Server product is not just a database; it also contains (as part of the product) an enterprise ETL tool (SQL Server Integration Services or SSIS), a Reporting Server, an OLAP and data mining server (Analysis Services), and several messaging technologies, specifically Service Broker and Notification Services.

Description

MS SQL Server uses a variant of SQL called T-SQL, or Transact-SQL, an implementation of SQL-92 (the ISO standard for SQL, certified in 1992) with some extensions. T-SQL mainly adds additional syntax for use in stored procedures, and affects the syntax of transaction support. (Note that SQL standards require Atomic, Consistent, Isolated, Durable or "ACID" transactions.) MS SQL Server and Sybase/ASE both communicate over networks using an application-level protocol called Tabular Data Stream (TDS). The TDS protocol has also been implemented by the FreeTDS project in order to allow more kinds of client applications to communicate with MS SQL Server and Sybase databases. MS SQL Server also supports Open Database Connectivity (ODBC).

SQL Server Express Edition

Formerly known as MSDE, Microsoft SQL Server Express is Microsoft's freely -downloadable and distributable version of its database engine that offers a database solution specifically targeted for embedded and smaller-scale applications. This version of the server contains some technical restrictions that make it unsuited for large-scale or production deployments; however, unlike its predecessor MSDE, there is no concurrent workload governor, which limited "performance if the database engine receives more work than is typical of a small number of users."

Most notable restrictions:

Maximum database size of 4 GB per database (compared to 2 GB in the former MSDE). The 4 GB limit is per database (log files excluded) and can be extended in some scenarios through the use of multiple interconnected databases.

Hardware utilization limits:

Single CPU
1 GB of RAM.
Absence of SQL Server Agent Service

Although its predecessor, MSDE, was virtually devoid of basic GUI management tools, the 2005 Express version now includes several GUI tools for database management. Among these tools are:

SQL Server Configuration Manager
SQL Server Management Studio Express
SQL Server Surface Area Configuration tool
SQL Server Business Intelligence Development Studio.

A relatively late addition to the SQL Server Express product line is a reduced functionality version of SQL Server Reporting Services. Although the addition of Reporting Services significantly expands the "out-of-the-box" functionality of the SQL Server Express product, enterprise features such as Analysis Services, Data Transformation Services, and Notification Services are only available in the "Standard" version and above.

Benefits

SQL Server 2000 XML Stored Procedure support:
Allows database developers to utilize XML immediately.

SQL Server 2000 XML Update Grams:
Allows developers to insert, update, and delete data in SQL Server 2000 with XML.

SQL Server 2000 Large Memory and SMP support:
Provides support for up to 32 CPUs and 64GB of RAM on Windows 2000 Data Center Edition for handling high transactional loads common in Web applications.

SQL Server 2000 Integrated Data Mining:
Uses data from large data sets to find hidden patterns and
trends.
SQL Server 2000 Distributed Partitioned Views:
Provides unlimited scalability by allowing work load to be
distributed across and processed by multiple servers in unison.

SQL Server 2000 Indexed (Materialized) Views:
Improves performance and scalability by storing and updating
calculated results on disk.

SQL Server 2000 Integrated Analysis Services:
The foundation for Online Analytical Processing (OLAP) and
data mining is included and fully integrated with SQL Server.
Competing database vendors require customers to purchase this
capability as an expensive add-on.

SQL Server 2000 Dynamic Self-Management and Tuning:
Saves time and effort by automating complex tuning tasks.
Provides higher database availability by allowing administrators
to perform database management tasks while the database
remains online.

Question 01: Getting the Matching Records

I have tables A and B in Enterprise Manager. I need to get a column from A and then scan the entire contents of B to see whether the content value from the column in A actually exists in column B. How can I achieve this?

A: If you want to get only matching records, here's the code:

```
SELECT TableA.*, TableB.*

FROM TableA

INNER JOIN TableB ON TableA.ColumnYouWantToCheck =

TableB.ColumnYouWantToSearch
```

If you want to get all records from TableA and matching records from TableB, here's the code:

```
SELECT TableA.*, TableB.*

FROM TableA

LEFT JOIN TableB ON TableA.ColumnYouWantToCheck =

TableB.ColumnYouWantToSearch
```

Note: If table B has no matching records, all fields selected from tableB will be null.

Question 02: Passing a Variable in a Different Field

I have a procedure like the following, but it doesn't work:

```
CREATE PROCEDURE GetFieldPath @FieldName varchar
(10), @ReturnField

Varchar (10) output

 AS

Select @ReturnField=@FieldName FROM TblPath
```

I want to have the field as a variable to pass it through a different field. Which part of the code went wrong?

A: Try this instead:

```
CREATE PROCEDURE GetFieldPath

@FieldName varchar (10),

@ReturnField varchar (10) output

AS

DECLARE @lcSQL nvarchar (300)

SET @lcSQL = 'SELECT @MyReturnField = '+@FieldName+'
FROM TblPath'

--- Change the type of parameter to match you needs

EXEC sp_executesql @lcSQL, N'@MyReturnField varchar
(10) OUTPUT',

@MyReturnField = @ReturnField OUTPUT

SELECT @ReturnField
```

Question 03: Date Formatting

I have a table that contains a column which is a datetime column, and contains dates in the format dd/mm/yy hh:mm:ss.

I am using a stored procedure to select the dates from this table. I want to format them differently and the stored procedure to change the formatting of the dates to mm/dd/yy hh:mm:ss.

I dont want to change them in the database, just the format they are returned in from this one stored procedure. Is this possible?

A: Yes it is possible. You can achieve this by doing the following:

```
Select   CONVERT (varchar (30), getdate (), 09) as
'mon dd yyyy

hh:mi:ss:mmmAM (or PM)'

Select   CONVERT (varchar (10), getdate (), 101) as
'mm/dd/yyyy'

Select   CONVERT (varchar (8), getdate (), 108) as
'hh:mm:ss'

Select   CONVERT (varchar (10), getdate (), 101) + '
' +

CONVERT (varchar (8), getdate (), 108) as 'mm/dd/yyyy
hh:mm:ss'
```

Question 04: Selecting Multiple Tables

I'm trying to SELECT * FROM 4 different tables where (DueDate < Today'sDate), and therefore reflect any overdues. I would like to display all of this information in a WebGrid and have the last column marked "Days Overdue".

I have a User Function created that will return the number of days overdue (posted at bottom) and return a column of "Total". I need to send this function to the due date for each of the rows within their respective tables.

How do I send all of the due dates to this function and make it work? Is there a better way to go about this? Here's the Theoretical SQL Statement:

```
SELECT dbo.Table1.Document name, dbo.Table2.Document
name,

dbo.Table3.Document name, dbo.Table4.Document name,

dbo.OverdueFunction(Currentdate, DUEDATES) as "Days
Overdue"

FROM dbo.Table1, dbo.Table2, dbo.Table3, dbo.Table4

WHERE DueDates < Today's Date

Function:

CREATE FUNCTION [dbo].[TotalOverDue]

(@CurrentDate as DateTime,

@DueDate as DateTime)

RETURNS  varchar(50)

BEGIN

DECLARE @TotalOverDue as Integer

DECLARE @HourTotal as Integer

DECLARE @NetTimeOverdue as Varchar(50)
```

```
SET @TotalOverDue =
DATEDIFF(minute,@CurrentDate,@DueDate)

SET @HourTotal=(@TotalOverDue/60)/24

SET @NetTimeOverdue = Cast((@HourTotal) as
varchar(10)) + ' Days '

RETURN   @NetTimeOverdue

END
```

A: Here's the Function:

```
CREATE FUNCTION [dbo].[TotalOverDue]

(@CurrentDate as DateTime,

@DueDate as DateTime)

RETURNS   varchar(50)

BEGIN

DECLARE @TotalOverDue as Integer

DECLARE @HourTotal as Integer

DECLARE @NetTimeOverdue as Varchar(50)

SET @TotalOverDue =
DATEDIFF(minute,@CurrentDate,@DueDate)

SET @HourTotal=abs((@TotalOverDue/60)/24)

SET @NetTimeOverdue = Cast((@HourTotal) as
varchar(10)) + ' Days '

RETURN   @NetTimeOverdue

END
Sql statement (for just 2 tables)
CODE:

SELECT dbo.CSS.DisplayName,

dbo.TotalOverDue(GetDate(), DateDue) as [Days
Overdue]
```

```
From     dbo.CSS

Where    DateDue < GetDate()

Union All

Select dbo.MSR.DisplayName,

dbo.TotalOverDue(GetDate(), DateDue) as [Days
Overdue]

From     dbo.MSR

Where    DateDue < GetDate()
```

Question 05: Moving Data From One Table to Another

I need to move a data from one table to another. The two tables have identical structures.

```
INSERT INTO Table 2 SELECT * FROM Table 1
```

However, one column needs to change. Is there a way to plug in this new value during the INSERT INTO statement or am I stuck having to update every row that was inserted? For example:

Table 1 has the following column values:

1. `4/1/2006 8:01:56 AM`

2. `15000`

3. `20000`

Table 2 needs to have:

1. `4/1/2006 8:00:00 A.M`

2. `15000`

3. `20000`

A: You can try this instead:

```
INSERT INTO Table2

SELECT convert (DateTime,'20060401'), field2, field3,
<rest of fields here>

FROM Table1
```

Question 06: Updating a Record Without Using a Cursor

I have a table called "Appointments" with the following data:

Rec_id	ApptDate	BeginTime	SlotDur	ProviderDur
1	20060430	1000	20	20
2	20060501	1020	20	40
3	20060501	1040	20	
4	20060502	1000	20	60
5	20060502	1020	20	
6	20060502	1040	20	

What this means, for example, is that each record has a 20 minute slot (BeginTime). If an appointment takes 20 minutes, it takes up 1 20 minute slot (Rec_id = 1) and populates the ProviderDur field with 20.

But if a patient makes an appointment that will last 40 minutes (ProviderDur) (Red_ID = 2 and 3 (two slots)) Rec_id Number 2's ProviderDur is populated with 40 but Rec_id Number 3's ProviderDur is null.

Is there a way to populate the null record with 20 if the record before = 40? This is part of a very large stored procedure that takes a while to run and a cursor which will make it even worse.

A: Try the code below to populate the null record.

```
create table testable

(Rec_id        int,

ApptDate       varchar(8),

BeginTime   varchar(4),

SlotDur     int,

ProviderDur int

)
insert into testTable values(1,'20060430', '1000',
20,20)

insert into testTable values(2,'20060501', '1020',
20,40)

insert into testTable values(3,'20060501', '1040',
20,null)

insert into testTable values(4,'20060502', '1000',
20,60)

insert into testTable values(5,'20060502', '1020',
20,null)

insert into testTable values(6,'20060502', '1040',
20,null)

select * from testable

declare @CurrentValue int

SET @CurrentValue = 0

UPDATE testable
```

```
SET ProviderDur = CASE WHEN ProviderDur IS NULL THEN
@CurrentValue ELSE

ProviderDur END,

@CurrentValue = CASE WHEN @CurrentValue > 20 THEN
@CurrentValue - 20

ELSE ProviderDur END

Select * from testTable
```

Question 07: Primary Key ID

Is there anyway of getting the primary key ID of a record that was inserted via stored procedure? I currently use:

```
CREATE PROCEDURE strInsertRecord

@value1 varchar (50),

@value2 varchar (50),

@NewRecordID int OUTPUT

AS

INSERT INTO MyTable (Field1, Field2) VALUES (@value1,
@value2)

SET @NewRecordID = (SELECT MAX (PrimaryKeyID) FROM
MyTable)

RETURN
```

I'm going to use @@IDENTITY since I'm using SQL Server 7.0.

A: If your "PrimaryKeyID" and identity is in column, return the value of:

```
SCOPE_IDENTITY( ).
```

Question 08: SQL Table

I have the SQL table that provides a Batch_Number and number of cycles that the transaction will run every month. For some reason, the Batch is not running because the number of cycles was changed to 0. I need to run an audit to see who, when, why, and how it was changed.

A: If this is data related change, you can try and get a transaction log explorer such as one provided by luminent.

I don't think you will be able to determine who made this change unless your application does internal auditing or you have auditing via SQL profiler.

I suggest setting your users and roles/profiles so as to stop anyone doing direct updates to your data unless authorized to do so.

Question 09: Instance Size

I used sp_helpdb and it shows size of each database. Is there a way to automatically sum up those values?

The ideal is to see that result divided in data and logs. I checked master..sysdatabases and master..sysfiles, but it's not useful. How can I get the size of a whole instance?

A: You can capture the output of a system stored procedure by creating a temp table and then using Insert/Exec. Like this:

```
Create

Table  #Temp (

Name VarChar(100),

db_Size VarChar(100),

Owner VarChar(100),

dbid int,
```

```
        Created DateTime,

        Status VarChar(1000),

        Compatibility_level int)
Insert Into #Temp Exec sp_helpdb

Select Sum(convert(decimal(10,4), Replace(db_size,
'MB', ''))) From #Temp

Drop Table #Temp
```

Question 10: Combining Two Tables and a View

I'm having a problem combining two tables consisting of one table and a view. I want all values from the first table, with a count from a second table, if rows do exist. If not, I want 0.

crm_reasons:

crm_reason_id	complaint
1	y
2	n
3	y
4	y
5	n

crm_ir_with_calldate:

crm_reason_id	crm_interaction_id	date_called
...		
2	100	2006-04-01 12:00:00
3	101	2006-04-02 12:00:00
5	101	2006-04-02 12:00:00

| 4 | 102 | 2006-04-03 12:00:00 |
| 3 | 103 | 2006-04-04 12:00:00 |

...

TSQL:

```
SELECT r.crm_reason_id, if(COUNT(ir.crm_reason_id) IS
NOT NULL,

COUNT(ir.crm_reason_id), 0) AS count

FROM crm_reasons r

LEFT OUTER JOIN crm_ir_with_calldate ir ON
r.crm_reason_id =

ir.crm_reason_id

WHERE r.complaint = 'y'

AND ir.date_called BETWEEN '2006-04-01' AND '2006-04-
25 23:59:59'

GROUP BY r.crm_reason_id

ORDER BY r.crm_reason_id
```

Should yield:

```
crm_reason_id count
     1            0
     3            2
     4            1
```

But instead, I get:

CODE:

```
crm_reason_id count
     3            2
     4            1
```

What did I do wrong? What course of action do I have?

A: A where clause condition involving a column from the right table in a left outer join effectively turns the query into an inner join.

When there's an unmatched row from the right table, then all the columns from the right table are null in that row of the results.

But if you have a where clause on it, then the null can't be equal to anything, nor can it be between any two values, so that unmatched row is filtered out.

The solution for this is that you have to move the condition into the ON clause, thus it becomes part of the join condition, which determines the match.

```
SELECT r.crm_reason_id

, COUNT(ir.crm_reason_id) as ir_count

LEFT OUTER

JOIN crm_ir_with_calldate ir

ON r.crm_reason_id = ir.crm_reason_id

AND ir.date_called

BETWEEN '2006-04-01'

AND '2006-04-25 23:59:59'

WHERE r.complaint = 'y'

GROUP

BY r.crm_reason_id

ORDER

BY r.crm_reason_id
```

Question 11: Running SQL Server

My SQL Server just stopped all by itself and generated an error #1069 stating that the service did not start due to log on failure occurred while performing this service operaton on the MS SQL Server service.

How do I get my SQL server running again?

A: This is caused by either the SQL Server or SQL Agent not being able to log on. The password may have been changed.

In the Enterprise manager, right click on "Your Server" and also on SQL Agent to find out what they are trying to logon as.

You can change this password by:

1. Open up Control Panel

2. Double-click Services, and then double-click MSSQLSERVER.

3. Type the correct password in the Password and Confirm password textbox, and then click ok.

Question 12: SQL server 7 Database

What tools do I need to create a WWW front-end/interface for an SQL Server 7 database? I need to make a secure intranet that allows a select 20 clients to login to a database from remote locations via Internet Explorer or Netscape and interract with it.

Are such tools included with MS SQL Server 2000? And if I purchase SQL Server 7 or 2000 with a 25 client/CAL license, are all of the tools included to develop a database, tables, queries, forms, etc.?

If so, why is there a Developer Edition of SQL Server as well? What version of SQL Server comes with Visual Studio 6?

A: "Secure Intranet" doesn't have anything to do with a web server or SQL Server.

You can create secure pages in IIS using Domain accounts fairly easily and both Internet Explorer and Netscape support the login dialog boxes natively. Interacting with the database can be done using OLE DB / ADO connections from ASP pages.

You have quite a wide variety of techniques and designs you can use even more if you use the new NET servers and NET Visual Studio.

Question 13: Updating Two or More Tables

I have two tables, table1 and table 2 which both are having a unique identity column.

I have to update column A in table 1 with column B table 2 by using the unique identity column, as the join and having a where column C is blah.

How do I update when there are 2 or more tables joining?

A: Try the following:

```
UPDATE Table1 SET Column_A = Table2.Column_B

FROM Table1

INNER JOIN Table2 ON Table1.PK = Table2.FK

WHERE Table1.ColumnC = blah
```

Question 14: Deleting a Particular Database

I tried to delete a particular database and I get an "Error 3724: cannot drop database 'Encore' because it's published for replication". Does someone know where I can un-publish this so I can delete it?

A: In Enterprise Manager select Tools >> Replication.

The easier way is through the scratchpad.

Click on "replicate data" and then click on "remove replication". This will enable you to delete the unwanted files.

Question 15: Range Search Queries

How can I improve the performance of range search queries?

A: You can do a nice little trick that can make a great big difference in query performance.

Sometimes, SQL Server fails to use an existing table index when processing a query that does a range search. For example, if the search criteria in a query are like one of the following and ColData has a non-clustered index, SQL server may not use the index.

Where ColData between 'Z21' and 'Z47'

Where ColData>='Z21' And ColData<='Z47'

It is possible to force SQL Server to use the index by adding an optimizer hint to the query (for example, Index=IndxColData). We can also cause SQL Server to use the index by adding additional criteria to the query as shown below.

Where ColData Between 'Z21' and 'Z47'

 And ColData=ColData

Why add the criteria ColData=ColData? The idea here is to trick the query optimizer into using the correct index. The query optimizer almost always chooses to use an existing index for an equality search whereas it may not choose the index for a range search on the same column.

Note that the second condition is always true regardless of the records chosen. In fact, the Query Optimizer recognizes that the condition is always true and doesn't include it in the final query execution plan.

Question 16: Granting View Permissions

How can I grant view stored procedure permissions to a user in the database? I would like the user to see all the stored procedures in the database which will not change them in any way.

I have determined I can use this statement to accomplish this task:

```
GRANT VIEW DEFINITION ON OBJECT::
DatabaseNAME.usp_StoredProc

TO User;

GO
```

Do I have to run this statement for each stored procedure? Is there a single statement I can use? For example: using "ALL" or something?

A: You need to use that statement once for each procedure. You can, however, grant view definition rights to the schema that the objects are in. This will allow the user to see the definition of all objects in the schema.

If all the stored procedures are owned by dbo, for example, you need only to grant permissions to view the dbo schema. Here's an example on how to do this:

```
GRANT VIEW DEFINITION ON SCHEMA ::[{ SchemaName}] TO
[{UserName}]
```

Question 17: Calculation Across Tables

I'm having problems with a calcualtion across two tables. Here's how I did it:

```
update salesperformance

set salesperformance.Yr1RYTD = (COALESCE
salesperformance.yr1running,0) -

COALESCE(salesperformance.yr2running,0) +
buildsalesperformance.yeartotal)

from salesperformance

left outer join buildsalesperformance on

salesperformance.br_no=buildsalesperformance.br_no

where buildsalesperformance.yr=right(@latestyear -
1,2)

or in simpler terms

set column = tableA.value1 - tableA.value2 +
table2.value1
```

I am using COALESCE to prevent a null value from stopping the calculation. The problem is that the select to get table2.value1 is returning to no data as the data doesn't exist in table2.

What I want SQL to do is in the above case continue the calculation but substitute table2.value1 with 0 (zero). As soon as the filter finds no results in table2 the calculation stops.

A: You can check the code below if it works for you.

```
update salesperformance

set salesperformance.Yr1RYTD =

(COALESCE (salesperformance.yr1running,0) -

COALESCE (salesperformance.yr2running,0) +

buildsalesperformance.yeartotal)
```

```
from salesperformance

left join buildsalesperformance on

salesperformance.br_no    =
buildsalesperformance.br_no

AND buildsalesperformance.yr = right(@latestyear -
1,2)
```

Question 18: Deleting Duplicates From a Table

I came across this code to delete duplicate rows from a table in SQL 2000. I have tested it and it seems to do the trick, but I don't understand how it does it.

There is a table with a unique field, in this case [EmployeeID], and then we have numerous other columns that we want to check for duplicates and then delete the entire rows/s.

```
Delete table_name

where [EmployeeID] not in

(select min([EmployeeID]) from table_name

group by column1, column2, etc);
```

Can anyone explain how it does it? As I mentioned I have tested it on small sample data, but now I would like to implement it on live data (circa 30 million rows)

A: If you would run the inner select statement:

```
SELECT MIN ([employeeID]) FROM table_name

        GROUP BY column1, column2
```

Or let's say the following table:

```
employeeID      column1      column2
```

1	John	Smith
2	Marc	Jones
3	John	Smith

The GROUP BY section would cause the following grouping to occur (internally):

```
group 1
```

employeeID	column1	column2
1	John	Smith
3	John	Smith

```
group 2
```

employeeID	column1	column2
2	Marc	Jones

then the MIN(EmployeeID) would return (per group):

```
group 1
```

employeeID	column1	column2
1	John	Smith
3	John	Smith

```
=> MIN(employeeID) = 1
```

```
group 2
```

employeeID	column1	column2
2	Marc	Jones

```
=> MIN (employeeID) = 2
```

So the result of the statement would be:

```
EmployeeID
```

1

2

Now:

```
DELETE table_name

WHERE [EmployeeID] NOT IN

(SELECT MIN ([EmployeeID]) FROM table_name

GROUP BY column1, column2);
```

Is actually:

```
DELETE table_name

WHERE [EmployeeID] NOT IN (1, 2);
```

Which logically result in deleting the row with employee ID 3.

Question 19: Updating Data

I'm using SQL 2000. I have a database in my office and a database with my webhost. Is there anyway that I could set up SQL 2000 to update my office database and vice versa when the databases are updated?

Example 1: I get a new user on my webpage to sign up. I want that information to be transfered to my office database as well.

Example 2: I add a new product in my offfice d atabase and I want the webpage to be updated.

I don't mind if it has to be done only once a day like a scheduled task, but is this function done by any software for a database?

A: You should be able to do this via a trigger on each table. As you insert or update information on either table the other is automatically updated. Your SQL manual should tell you the commands to do this, especially if they are on different servers.

Another way is with replication. You can set up the replication in a way that once a day every new or changed data on one server is send to the other.

For replication it is necessary that it is impossible that your Office Database cannot change records and the WebDB can change them also. Only one of them may change the data of a range of data in a table.

It is the same for appending records. When both will append and they use the same Primary key numbers, the replication will fail. So make sure if both can append that they both have their one range of IDs.

Question 20: Updating Table1 with Contents from Table2

I have two tables:

Table1

Name	Number	UserID
James Jimmy	E1255	<NULL>
Jones Tom	E8544	<NULL>
Loeb Lisa	E9988	<NULL>

Table2

UserID	FirstName	LastName
12	Jimmy	James
55	Tom	Jones
49	Lisa	Loeb

I need to update Table1.UserID with Table2.UserID, matching Table1.Name to Table2.LastName + ' ' + Table2.FirstName. The subquery returned more than 1 value. Do you have any idea how to build this?

A: Use the following code:

```
Update Table1

Set     UserId = Table2.UserId

From    Table1

Inner Join Table2

On Table1.Name = Table2.LastName + ' ' +
Table2.FirstName
```

Please take note that you should make a backup of your database before continuing. You also have to check if there are no duplicates in the table.

Question 21: Creating a Report

I have a table with the following fields:

```
custid  int

canceldate  datetime
```

I need to create a report that will group the number of customer IDs found for a given month/date combination in the cancel date field. It needs to look something like this:

```
# customers cancelled    Month/year

        10                      Jan 2006

         2                      Feb 2006

         0                      Mar 2006
```

How should I do this?

A: Try the following:

```
select
count(custid),datename(month,canceldate),datename(yea
r,canceldate)

from table1

group by
datename(month,canceldate),datename(year,canceldate)
```

Question 22: Listing Columns in Order

I have this SQL code:

```
Select  Column_Name

From    Information_schema.columns

Where   Table_Name = 'IndEtioOutcomesDetail'

ORDER BY XXXX
```

Is there a way to order it so they show as they are in Design view?

A: Do the following:

```
Select  Column_Name

From    Information_schema.columns

Where   Table_Name = 'IndEtioOutcomesDetail'

ORDER BY ordinal_position
```

Question 23: Query Based on Select Records of Table1

I've included a small sample of the data I need to work with below:

TABLE1:

ID1	ID2	SEQ	TYPE	AMOUNT	USER_ID	INSERT_DT
810	1	1	D	100	BOB	05/07/2003
810	1	1	A	200	JANE	04/01/2004
17879	2	1	D	1250	BOB	07/04/2006
17879	2	1	A	1000	BOB	08/05/2006
17879	2	2	D	1000	BOB	08/07/2006
17879	2	2	A	800	JANE	08/08/2006
17879	6	1	D	2500	BOB	08/25/2006
17879	6	1	A	2000	BOB	08/25/2006
30578	3	1	D	500	BOB	06/16/2006
32651	4	1	V	1548	BOB	04/05/2005
41865	5	1	D	600	JANE	02/01/2005

This is what I would like to see in my resulting dataset:

ID1	OLD_AMOUNT	NEW_AMOUNT	USER	DATE

810	100	200
JANE	5/7/03	
17879	1250	1000
BOB	1/3/03	
17879	1000	800
JANE	5/27/03	

I need to find the records where there is a D and an A record for an ID that have the same ID1, ID2, and SEQ as each other, but the amount is different between them. I want the USER and DATE from the A record type, but I need the amounts from both the D and the A.

Notice that ID 17879 in TABLE1 has three D and A record groups (3 different ID1/ID2/SEQ concatenations), but the amount only changes in the first two, so I don't need the 3rd one returned.

Can this be done without creating temporary tables? I want to use this data for a Crystal Report so I can't create and drop temporary tables every time the report is run.

It would be great if I could also return all the records where the TYPE = 'V' as part of the same query. I could take a NULL value for the New Amount and stick the AMOUNT for the 'V' record in the Old Amount field. I've changed TABLE1 to have all of the required fields so I won't need to join to another.

A: I don't see why all 3 records shouldn't be returned for id1 = 17879.

For the rest, this should work:

```
"And A.AMOUNT <> B.AMOUNT"

Select A.Id1,

B.Amount,

A.Amount,

A.UserID,

A.Insert_DT
```

```
From    TableName A

Inner Join TableName B

    On A.ID1 = B.ID1

And A.ID2 = B.ID2

And A.SEQ = B.SEQ

And A.Type = 'A'

And B.Type = 'D'

Union All

Select ID1, NULL, Amount, UserId, Insert_DT

From    TableName
Where Type = 'V'
```

When joining a table to itself (commonly referred to as a Self Join), you need to use table aliases (the A and B parts).

There is a difference between union and union all. A union will combine 2 queries in to 1 but will perform a DISTINCT for you in the background.

Union ALL will allow you to have duplicate rows. Union ALL is faster than Union. Since you are filtering on Type, you don't need Union, which is why I used union all.

Moving forward, it's important that you understand the difference between union and union all.

Question 24: Returning Number of Records

I need to pull only 20 first rows of records from this select for testing. How can I do this?

```
Select a.firm_id,b.office_id,b.C_name,b.C_city

From

firm a,office b

where

b.firm_id = a.firm_id

order by a.firm_id
```

A: Do the following:

```
Select TOP 20 a.firm_id,b.office_id,b.C_name,b.C_city

From

firm a,office b

where

b.firm_id = a.firm_id
```

Question 25: Replacing Function in MsSQL

I've recently migrated from MySQL to MsSQL and just noticed a little break in my application with a query. The query used to work in MySQL is somthing like this:

```
<cfquery name="qImportStatistics"
datasource="#application.dsn#">

REPLACE tblUnitReports (unitID,

createdDate,

createdTime,

sentOK, and so on....
```

This searches the table against a 'unique' index and if a record for the unit and the current hour exists, it will just update it rather than inserting a new record.

But if no record for the current hour exists, it creates a new one as if it were an insert. And if I run the code on SQL, I get a syntax error but if a change it back to a standard INSERT then it works fine.

How can I replicate the MySQL REPLACE function into MsSQL? Can I use that If/Else in the SQL code and have the SQL Server do the work or should I be coding that with my Server Side code?

A: If you are looking for upsert however, that doesn't exist in SQL server (yet) it is on the request list.

For now, you have to do something like this:

```
if exists (select * from table where.....)

update table.....

else

insert table values()
```

For your second question, the answer is yes. You can use that in SQL code and have the server do the work. Here is an example, run it in a query analyzer to understand how it works:

```
create table abc (id int primary key,col2
varchar(50))

insert abc values(1,'123')

if exists (select * from abc where id = 1)
begin

update abc

set col2 ='xyz'

where id =1

end

else

begin

insert abc values(1,'xyz')

end

select * from abc

if exists (select * from abc where id = 2)

begin

update abc

set col2 ='aaa'

where id =2

end

else

begin

insert abc values(2,'aaa')
```

```
end

select * from abc
```

Consider using stored procedures since it will be much easier to maintain and execution plans can be re-used.

Question 26: DateDiff Function

I have two fields [Time_In] and [Time_Out] as smalldatetime fields. I'm trying to compute the total hours worked. I'm using the datediff function but it always returns an integer. So, if a person worked 7.5 hours, it would return as 7.

```
DateDiff (hour, [Time_In], [Time_Out])
```

What I want to do is return a decimal to one digit such as 7.5, 8.0, etc. I tried casting this to float and decimal datatypes but to no avail. How c an I resolve this?

A: Use the following code:

```
CONVERT (real, DATEDIFF (minute, Time_In, Time_Out)

/ 60.0) As DailyHours
```

Use real instead of decimal because it's a smaller datatype, although less precise. In the front end application, just format it to two digits.

Question 27: Adding Numeric Value

I want to update a table by adding a value from one table into a table that currently contains Null. How c an I do this?

```
UPDATE table1

SET NrofRows = a.NrOfRows + b.NrOfRows

FROM table1 a, table2 b

WHERE a.Key = b.Key

The Values contained are

table1 NrOfRows = Null

table2 NrOrRows = 1000
```

A: Here's the Code:

```
UPDATE table1

SET NrofRows = coalesce(a.NrOfRows,0) +
coalesce(b.NrOfRows,0)

FROM table1 a, table2 b

WHERE a.Key = b.Key
```

Question 28: Finding Duplicate Rows

I'm trying to find the duplicate rows between 2 tables. The unique index for tblOrders is across 7 columns:

```
AcctNatl, AcctBillTo, UPC, Title, Artist,
campaignCode, OrderDtm
```

Insert from tblOrdersImport into tblOrders fails with "duplicate key" error. Yet, when I run this SQL stmt, it returns 0 rows:

```
SELECT        *

FROM          dbo.tblOrders INNER JOIN
dbo.tblOrdersImport ON

              dbo.tblOrders.AcctNatl =
dbo.tblOrdersImport.AcctNatl

              AND dbo.tblOrders.AcctBillTo =
dbo.tblOrdersImport.AcctBillTo

              AND dbo.tblOrders.UPC =
dbo.tblOrdersImport.UPC

              AND dbo.tblOrders.Title =
dbo.tblOrdersImport.Title

              AND dbo.tblOrders.Artist =
dbo.tblOrdersImport.Artist

              AND dbo.tblOrders.campaignCode =

              dbo.tblOrdersImport.CampaignCode

              AND dbo.tblOrders.orderDtm =
dbo.tblOrdersImport.OrderDtm
```

How can I construct the SQL statement to find the duplicate records?

A: The problem is that you have duplicates in the tblOrdersImport table.

```
run this
```

```
select AcctNatl, AcctBillTo, UPC, Title, Artist,
campaignCode, OrderDtm

from tblOrdersImport

group by AcctNatl, AcctBillTo, UPC, Title, Artist,
campaignCode, OrderDtm

having count(*) >1
```

Question 29: Migrating from Sybase to SQL Server 6.5

How do I move some small Sybase (11.5.1) databases to MS SQL Server 6.5? Does it have any pros and cons of moving a database from Sybase to SQL Server?

A: You have to transfer to table structures and data manually.

If you build scripts for your tables, then it is much better, as the syntax should be virtually the same (SQL Server is Sybase ported to NT). If not, and your database schema is large, then get ErWin and use it to generate the build scripts for you.

Data can be transferred using bcp, syntax should be nearly the same except that SYBCHAR will now be VARCHAR.

Any stored procedures and triggers should also be almost the same, but may need some small syntactical changes.

It is mainly a case of 'give it a go'. If it is just tables and data then it won't be too hard. SPs may be slightly harder.

Question 30: USE Command

We have a number of SQL 7.0 databases where we want to perform the same task on each one, so we have written a stored procedure to perform the task.

The stored procedure uses a USE command to point it at the appropriate database (defaulting to master), which it obtains from a cursor which extracts the database names from sysdatabases. However, when the database name is placed into a variable and then the variable passed to the USE command it doesn't work.

For example, USE @DB_Name doesn't do anything.

If the EXEC method 'EXEC ("USE " + @DB_Name)' function is used, it works fine but once the EXEC has completed, the database returns to the default database and any subsequent refrences to DB_Name use Master. How can I achieve this sort of routine? What am I doing wrong?

A: You should use the undocumented stored procedure sp_msforeachdb. It is much easier. Here is an article from the internet about it:

sp_MSForEachDB

SQL Server includes an un-documented stored procedure that can make performing on the fly tasks against all databases on a single server easier. This command should never be used in a production environment but can be of use for quickly executing code in a development or test environment.

The procedure uses a cursor to loop through the sysdatabases table and execute an inputted command against each database on that system. While this would be a fairly trival task for someone to write, this procedure already exists so can save you time for those one off tasks.

At a basic level you can simply execute this stored procedure with a TSQL command as a parameter. Place A where the database name should be located.

e.g., Run the DBCC command against every database on the server.

```
exec sp_MSForEachDB 'DBCC CheckDB(?)'
```

Or quickly backup all databases on a server.

```
exec sp_MSForEachDB "backup database ? to
DISK='c:\winnt\temp\?.bak'"
```

Note: You are likely to get an error stating TempDB cannot be backed up. As TempDB is recreated from model each time the server is restarted this can safely be ignored.

However, the functionality of this stored procedure doesn't end here. The parameters to the procedure are as follows:

```
sp_MSForEachDB <command1>,
<replacementcharacter>,<comand2>, <command3>,
<precommand>, <postcommand>
```

The <command> parameters are the TSQL command you wish to perform against each database and you can have three. The replacement character tells this stored procedure which character in the command strings are to be replaced with the name of each database and this defaults to "?". The <precommand> is a command to run before the other commands are executed against each database. The <postcommand> is run after the database commands have finished running against each database.

For example, show which database is being maintained, run the DBCC checkdb on the database, and then backup the database.

```
exec sp_MSForEachDB "select 'Performing Maintance for
DB: *'",'*','DBCC CheckDB(*)',"backup database * to
DISK='c:\winnt\temp\*.bak'"
```

Question 31: Viewing Selected Quarter and Previous Quarter

I have a table with the fields Year, Quarter, & Rate. My parameters to pass the query would be Year & Quarter. I need selected quarter, and previous quarter. So if I pass year-2000 and quarter-3, I need a final view that shows:

```
Year      Rate for Quarter3     rate for Quarter2
Difference in Rate
```

How can I do this?

A: If those are the only three fields in your table, you could add an [ID] field and subtract 1 from the [ID] corresponding to your specified year and quarter to get previous.

If you have different multiple entries for each year/qtr, create a lookup table that has an Identity field, year, and quarter. Then pass year and quarter into your query. This will allow it to get 'Rate for Quarter 3'.

You then could go to lookup table to get [ID] where year = 2000 and quarter = 3.

Then take this [ID]-1, go back to lookup table and get corresponding year, quarter to be used in retrieving 'Rate for Previous Quarter'

I assume your table looks something like:

Year	Quarter	Value
2004	1	9
2004	2	8
2004	3	7
2004	4	6
2005	1	5
2005	2	4
2005	3	3
2005	4	2
2006	1	1

Where the Value column would represent your rate column.

If you had some sort of incrementing ID for each quarter, then a simple self join would make this problem simple. However, since you have year and quarter, we need to get a little creative. Using pure T-SQL, we can manufacture an incrementing ID to accomplish this. Here's how:

We know that dates start on Jan 1, 1900. So, if we subtract 1900 from the year column and add it to the 0 date (Jan 1, 1900) we would effectively get Jan 1 of the year. Of course, this doesn't solve the problem, but don't stop reading either, because here's where it gets good.

Using T-SQL, we can also add a Quarter to a date. This will give us the first day of the quarter time for an example. You can copy/paste this code in to Query Analyzer and run the code to see how it works.

```
Declare @Temp Table(Year Integer, Quarter Integer,
Value Integer)

Insert Into @Temp Values(2004,1,9)

Insert Into @Temp Values(2004,2,8)

Insert Into @Temp Values(2004,3,7)

Insert Into @Temp Values(2004,4,6)

Insert Into @Temp Values(2005,1,5)

Insert Into @Temp Values(2005,2,4)

Insert Into @Temp Values(2005,3,3)

Insert Into @Temp Values(2005,4,2)

Insert Into @Temp Values(2006,1,1)

Select *, DateAdd(Quarter, Quarter-1, DateAdd(year,
year-1900, 0)) As

FirstDayInQuarter

From    @Temp
```

The results are:

Year	Quarter	Value	FirstDayInQuarter
2004 00:00:00.000	1	9	2004-01-01
2004 00:00:00.000	2	8	2004-04-01
2004 00:00:00.000	3	7	2004-07-01
2004 00:00:00.000	4	6	2004-10-01
2005 00:00:00.000	1	5	2005-01-01
2005 00:00:00.000	2	4	2005-04-01
2005 00:00:00.000	3	3	2005-07-01
2005 00:00:00.000	4	2	2005-10-01
2006 00:00:00.000	1	1	2006-01-01

We have manufactured a date the represents the first day of the quarter. We're getting closer, but we still have a little more work to do because using this newly manufactured column to do a self join would still be problematic. Using a little more SQL date magic, we can calculate the number of quarters that have elapsed between day 0 (Jan 1, 19000) and the manufactured date.

Using the same table variable in the previous example, copy/paste this code to see what I mean.

```
Select *, DateDiff(Quarter, 0, DateAdd(Quarter,
Quarter-1, DateAdd(year, year-1900, 0))) As
```

QuartersSinceJan1_1900

From   @Temp

Now we get:

Year	Quarter	Value	QuartersSinceJan1_1900
2004	1	9	416
2004	2	8	417
2004	3	7	418
2004	4	6	419
2005	1	5	420
2005	2	4	421
2005	3	3	422
2005	4	2	423
2006	1	1	424

Finally, we have manufactured an integer column that we can use to perform a self jo in. The self join and the where clause for your filter criteria would look something like this:

```
Select *, B.Value - A.Value As Difference

From    @Temp A

        Inner Join @Temp B On

            DateDiff(Quarter, 0, DateAdd(Quarter,
A.Quarter-1, DateAdd(year, A.year-

1900, 0)))

            = DateDiff(Quarter, 0, DateAdd(Quarter,
B.Quarter-1, DateAdd(year,

B.year-1900, 0))) + 1

Where   A.Year = 2005
```

```
        And A.Quarter = 1
```

The output:

```
Year Quarter Value Year Quarter Value Difference

---- ------- ----- ---- ------- ----- -----------

2005 1       5     2004 4       6     1
```

When you run this query, you'll notice that the difference in values is obtained even if we span years.

Question 32: Dynamic SELECT Statement in Stored Procedure

I'm creating a stored procedure for a report Web page which allows the user to specify different criteria. I need it to be able to dynamically build parts of the WHERE clause. Here's what I have so far:

```
CREATE PROC sp_survey_report

@business char(10),

@sub_business char(10),

@engagement_type char(8),

@full_part_time_ind char(3),

@comp_type char(3)

AS

IF @business = "ALL" SELECT @business = "%"

IF @sub_business = "ALL" SELECT @sub_business = "%"

IF @engagement_type = "ALL" SELECT @engagement_type = "%"
```

```
IF @full_part_time_ind = "ALL" SELECT
@full_part_time_ind = "%"

IF @comp_type = "ALL" SELECT @comp_type = "%"

SELECT COUNT(*)

FROM t_survey, t_survey_data

WHERE t_survey.survey_id = t_survey_data.survey_id

AND question_id = "1" AND response_value = "01"

AND business like @business

AND sub_business like @sub_business

AND engagement_type like @engagement_type

AND full_part_time_ind like
SUBSTRING(@full_part_time_ind, 1, 1)

AND comp_type like SUBSTRING(@comp_type, 1, 1)

... ;

('full_part_time_ind' and 'comp_type' are 1-character
columns in t_survey)
```

When I call the SP like this:

```
exec sp_survey_report "SUPPLY", "", "NHR", "F", "E";
I get the correct counts, but when I call the SP like
this
```

```
exec sp_survey_report "ALL", "ALL", "ALL", "ALL",
"ALL";
```

I get incorrect results. Why is this? Alternatively, I think the
following is possible:

```
CREATE PROCEDURE myProc

Blah

Blah

AS
```

```
DECLARE @command varchar(255)

SELECT @command = "SELECT COUNT(*) FROM blah blah..."

IF some_condition @command = @command + @something

EXEC @command

;
```

How can I get the COUNT returned from the executed SELECT statement?

A: The way to select all on your stored procedure is not to pass the word "ALL", that is being included in your where clause, and will only return rows that match (i.e., where business and sub-business are ALL etc).

You need to modify your where clause to use the "LIKE" command, then you can just pass a % into the stored procedure, and that should return all rows. And it's easier to build the correct SQL string before sending it to the database.

Maybe the following will work with strCriteria being the WHERE argument:

```
IF parameter1 condition...

THEN strCriteria = strCriteria & parameter1 & " AND "

IF parameter2 condition...

THEN strCriteria = strCriteria & parameter2 & " AND "

etc.

etc.

strCriteriaFinal = Left(strCriteria,
Len(strCriteria)-5)
sqltext = "SELECT blah, blah, FROM blah, blah WHERE
"& strCriteria
```

You can build the dynamic SQL in the SP as you've started and then use Execute or sp_executesql to execute the SQL string. You must also make sure you delimit the character or text fields with quotes.

```
DECLARE @sql varchar(1024)

Select @sql=

"SELECT COUNT(*)

FROM t_survey s Inner Join t_survey_data d

ON s.survey_id=d.survey_id

WHERE question_id = '1'

AND response_value = '01'

AND business like '" + @business + "'

AND sub_business like '" + @sub_business + "'

AND engagement_type like '" + @engagement_type + "'

AND full_part_time_ind like '" +
SUBSTRING(@full_part_time_ind, 1, 1) + "'

AND comp_type like '" + SUBSTRING(@comp_type, 1, 1) +
"'"

...;

Execute(@sql)
```

Question 33: Changing Integer to Decimal

I have SQL statement that I cannot get the precise values because it keeps rounding them. Can someone steer me as to what I'm doing wrong? Here is my code:

```
SELECT     SUM(QTY) AS Qty, CAST(DATEDIFF(wk,
MIN(DayDate), MAX(DayDate)) AS

decimal) AS NumWk, CAST(SUM(QTY) / DATEDIFF(wk,
MIN(DayDate),MAX(DayDate)) AS

decimal) AS AvgOrd FROM dbo.X850_VW
```

This is running a view off another view.

Expected Results	Actual
QTY: 220	220
NumWk: 38.86	39
AvgOrd: 5.66	6

A: Your problem is in here:

```
CAST (DATEDIFF (wk, MIN (DayDate), MAX (DayDate)) AS
decimal)
```

DateDiff always returns an integer. If you expect to get fractional numbers from date diff, then you need to change the interval and do a little math.

```
Convert (Decimal (10, 2), DATEDIFF (day, MIN
(DayDate), MAX (DayDate))) / 7.0
```

Question 34: Data From DTS to Access

I created a Stored Procedure which pulls data into a temporary (named - #temp) table and then selects "all" from the #temp table. All of the data is returned as it should and the proc "runs" as it should.

Then I created a DTS package with a connection from SQL and a connection "To an Access Database" with a "Transformation Data Task (TDT)" between the two.

On the source for the "TDT" I use query: "EXEC ReportProc". I can preview the query and get the data I saw when I ran the procedure in the query analyzer.

I cannot create a destination or any transformations – i.e., I cannot send the data to Access. I get the following error:

`Error Description: Invalid object name `#temp``

I figure this error occurs because this is a "temp" table and it is dropped after the PROC is run – however, that does not explain why I can get the data in the preview by executing the PROC but I still cannot drop the data into access.

Is there any way to gather data from a stored procedure, execute it in a DTS package, and then export it to Access from the DTS?

A: Yes there is a way. This is how you can fix it:

-Use Global vars (##)

-When you build a DTS package and call a SP (with a global var) from a box other than the machine that the DTS is on, the Global Var will not be recognize.

-Use an Execute SQL Task (Drop Table ##x) in the DTS, instead of in the SP. Execute at the end of the package.

Question 35: Identifying Databases in EM

My organization has several SQL databases. I can establish connections to them through Enterprise Manager by typing in their IP addresses in the NEW box and completing the wizard, but then under my SQL Group I end up with several databases identified only by their IP addresses.

Is there a way I could get EM to display a name for these databases like Sales, Marketing, and Production? Or is there a better way for me to establish the connection so I end up with a name instead?

A: Are you sure it's the databases showing up with IP addresses? When you register through Enterprise Manager, you are registering the SERVER, not the database(s). Then you expand on the server and that will show you the available database(s).

To show server names, you need to register the server with the name, not the IP and that will only work if you have DNS set up to resolve the names.

If your databases are specific per server (e.g., Sales DBs are nevever mixed with Marketing or Production on the same server, and the same for all 3 types), then you could numb the pain a bit by creating a SQL Server Group in EM and register each server in the appropriately named group.

Question 36: Field-level security

Is there any product/utility out there that offers field-level security? We have a front-end access project (adp) using a SQL server 2000 back-end.

A: You can set the field level security in SQL2000. Go to the security tab for a table and press the columns button.

Question 37: SQL Server Error with DELETE

I'm trying to delete entries out of a SQL table called FACTOID. It has three fields:

- FactoidID (datatype 'int'; Identity=1)
- DataFact ('ntext')
- ShowDate ('datetime')

My .ASP file contains the SQL Delete code:

```
sqltext="DELETE from factoid where DataFact='<text
value here>'"
    . . . . .
set record_pointer=connection_var.execute(sqltext)
```

I get the following ERROR:

The text, ntext, and image data types cannot be used in the WHERE, HAVING, or ON clause, except with the LIKE or IS NULL predicates.

I'm not exactly sure what this means. Is there a problem with my sql command or with how I defined my table columns?

A: Can you use a varchar for DataFact rather than ntext?

You can't use WHERE on an nText type for some weird, technical reason.

Question 38: Setting Varchar Dynamically

How can I set a variable with a dynamic query? Here is my code:

```
declare @Sql as varchar (8000)

declare @where as varchar (8000)

declare @rows as int

set @Sql = 'select count(*) from table '

set @where = ' where 1=1 and 2=2 '

set @rows = @Sql  + @where

print @rows
```

A: CODE:

```
declare @Sql as varchar (8000)

declare @where as varchar (8000)

declare @RowAffected as int

set @Sql = 'select count(*) from syscolumns '

set @where = ' where 1=1 and 2=2 '

exec (@Sql  + @where )

SET @RowAffected = @@RowCount

print @RowAffected

using sp_ExecuteSql would be my preferred method.
```

CODE:

```
--dyn vars

declare @parm1 integer,@table varchar(50)
```

```
set @parm1 = 0

set @table = 'syscolumns'

declare @sqlstm nvarchar(200), @parmlist
nvarchar(200)

set @sqlstm = 'select @parm1 = count(*) from ' +
@table

set @parmlist = '@parm1 integer OUTPUT'

exec sp_ExecuteSql @sqlstm, @parmlist, @parm1 OUTPUT

select @parm1 as numberofrows
```

Question 39: Creating a "Comment Key" Field

I created a view which contains a "CommentKey" field which is a combination of other fields within the table of all data types. The float (8) field is also converted to NVarChar, but the output for longer data is (for example) 1.056e+006 as opposed to 1056000.0. Here is the code:

```
select * ,

Cast (

ACCTG_RISK_REF+

TECH_TRAN_NUM+

TECH_TRAN_TYPE+

INSTAL_NO+

TECH_TRAN_VERSN+

ORIG_CCY_CODE+

UW_ACCOUNT_REF+

CLIENT_ACCOUNT_REF+
```

```
Cast (

UW_ORIG_NETT_AMT

as NVarChar (50))

as NVarChar (100))

as "CommentKey"

from dbo.O_BUREAU_EXTRACT_PPWEXTR
```

I would rather do away with the decimals all together.

How do I get rid of the decimal sections (for example round off)? How do I get 1056000.0 to display as 1056000 not as 1.056e+006? 1056000.0 is merely one example of thousands. How will a Set @Temp = 1056000.0 look generically?

A: The Set 'stuff' was for demonstration purposes to show that rounding, then converting to integer and finally to nvarchar would solve the problem.

This is what you should do: Replace the @Temp variable in the code I provided with the field (or field combinations) that you want converted.

```
select * ,

Cast (

ACCTG_RISK_REF+

TECH_TRAN_NUM+

TECH_TRAN_TYPE+

INSTAL_NO+

TECH_TRAN_VERSN+

ORIG_CCY_CODE+

UW_ACCOUNT_REF+
```

```
CLIENT_ACCOUNT_REF+

Cast (

Convert (INT, Round(UW_ORIG_NETT_AMT, 0))
as NVarChar (50))

as NVarChar (100))

as "CommentKey"

from dbo.O_BUREAU_EXTRACT_PPWEXTR
```

Question 40: Database From ASP Page

I'm having trouble connecting to a database from an ASP page. I'm getting the error: Not associated with a trusted SQL Server connection. What is wrong?

A: Your server is either set up to use only NT authentication rather than mixed-mode or standard authentication, OR your client (ADO, I assume) is trying to connect to the server using NT mode instead of standard mode, or both. Change it to accept both NT and SQL server authentication for you to make a connection.

Question 41: Executing a Stored Procedure

Is it possible to execute a store procedure from within a query? Here's an example of what I would like to do:

```
select emp_id, last_name, first_name,

        (exec sp_Get_Overall_Incentive_Score @emp_id
= em.emp_id) as score

    from employee_master as em

    where term = 0
```

A: From the looks of things what you really want to do is create a user defined function. You can create a UDF like this:

```
CREATE function dbo.getOverallScore (@emp_id int)
returns int
as begin

declare @Score int

select @Score = Avg(SingleScore)

from MyScoreData (nolock)

return @Score

end
```

Question 42: Access SQL Server through VPN

I am using Win2k and trying to connect to a SQL 7 server. I can connect to the network fine and do normal stuff but not with enterprise manager and SQL 7 . How to access an SQL server through vpn using Enterprise manager?

A: Without knowing the specifics of your connection or any messages, you might receive when attempting to connect. You need to change the Network Library used to connect to SQL Server. The default library is named pipes and it may not work over VPN.

Start the Client Network Utility and view the connection properties. You may or may not have a connection defined. If you don't have a connection defined, then create one and set the Network Library to TCP/IP or Multiprotocol.

If the connection exists, you may need to change the network library from named pipes to TCP/IP or multiprotocol. Make sure SQL Server can accept the protocol you choose.

If you've tried the available protocols with no success, try to ping your SQL server so you can know if it is reachable from your connection.

Question 43: Trigger Preventing Table Deletes

I need a trigger to prevent deletion of any rows on all tables except for those I specify. How do I make this work?

A: Put a column in your table that is called ReadOnly or something to that effect. Make is a bit data type. If it's not deleteable, set ReadOnly to 1.

Have a trigger on the table setup that checks t he max imum value of the ReadOnly field in the deleted column. If the value is 1 issue a rollback command.

Question 44: Duplicate Records in Two Tables

Are there duplicate records that are in two tables? The first table is called Contacts. The unique Identifier is usage_indicator and name. I tried doing this:

```
Delect ABMcontacts

where usage_indicator not in

(select min (usage_indicator)

from ABMcontacts group by usage_indicator, name)

and name not in

(select min (name)

from ABMcontacts group by usage_indicator, name)
```

This runs for over an hour and does not do anything. Is there a way to pull duplicate records based on the usage_indicator and name and delete then?

A: First, your query takes forever because for each record to check in the table ABMcontacts it will run the queries with the function MIN (...) FROM ... group by.

Secondly, the two queries always produce the same output each time you run it. MIN (...) is always the same because the queries don't have other search criteria.

To speed up your process, execute the subqueries apart and only give the end result to the query you described. The query will run a long time because both subqueries will run for every record in the table. For example, if the table has 10,000 rows, SQL Server will run each subquery 10,000 times.

You can identify the duplicates with this query:

```
Select usage_indicator, name, count (*) As cnt

From ABMcontacts

Group By usage_indicator, name

Having count (*) > 1
```

There is an excellent article on the SQLTeam website about deleting duplicates. It listed a few methods. You can choose the one that is best for you.

Question 45: SQL Server when Using DSL

We have installed a DSL. We do not want to obtain our TCP/IP addresses from the provider because we like our network to function even if the p rovider is down. We cannot connect to SQL 7.0 under this situation.

Right now we can disable DNS in network settings (on each workstation) and have the SQL 7.0, or enable DNS and have our connection to the net on the DSL.

Does anyone know how to set everything up so this will work?

A: If you have DSL, you have at least one address from them. You are probably using a router with Name Address Translation. You have to do two things.

Most routers with NAT (you may have to enlist the help of you ISP here) can pass requests off to another computer on a port by port basis.

You tell the router to pass requests to the correct port as SQL Server uses 1433 on to your SQL Server's IP like 192.168.0. or 10.0.0 .

To connect, you point the client to the address in the router. It looks like a SQL Server to the outside world. If the ISP uses DHCP to assign an address to your router, you have a problem. The address to which you connect from the outside may change.

Also, you can't be using named pipes to get at the SQL server over the internet. You probably figured thatyou didn't have it set for IP in the first place.

Question 46: Primary Key Change

The external factors are forcing me to change the Primary Key of my main table. The ID (Member_ID) is now only used for a segment of the business. The Member_ID field is the Foreign Key in multiple tables.

The goal is to make Member_ID an int (autonumber). I already created a new field and updated Member_ID1 (there is also a Member_ID2 which is forcing me into this situation) with the old Member_ID. How can I update the ID.?

A: If you have cascading update enabled on all the foreign key tables, you can change the main table and all the others will change.

If not, then you need to know exactly what tables are affected and change them first, then the main table. In this case you may need to temporarily disable referential integrity. For handling this, make a backup before you start.

Question 47: Setting up the Login Server

I finally got the service running but when I tried to connect to the server it will not accept a log in. During the install process, I never had the chance to set up an account for the server. I'm running WIN98 with website 2.3. How do I set up the login for the server?

I'm also just using the 'sa' with no password. My server comes up in the manager with the green arrow showing it is running, but when I click on it to show the folders a red wavy line appears right besides the green arrow. I can't find a reference to this to know if this is normal or not.

I have made sure the MSDTC, MSSQLServer and SQLServerAgent are all running. Also, I have TCP/IP as the library. My server shows up as "Stargazer" or (local). The DTS does the "find function" until you click the finished button. Then the entire manager and DTS locks up. How do I fix this?

A: Re-install windows and get every thing running but the DTS. The DTS goes through all the steps and gets to the last step with the 'finished' button. But it locks up there and will not import the data. Try to import an Access database to see how it works.

Then, check if the services are still on or not. You can do this from the control panel also. MSDTC services are required to perform this task. Correctly name the source and the destinations.

Secondly, select the connection drivers properly that enable you to do the data transfers. In the source, select the MS Access and the destinatio n should be MS OLE DB Provider for SQL Server.

Question 48: DTS Job

I've created a DTS job which will export data from a table into a text file using the delimited format. The field is a char datatype of size 10 chars. I need to be able to strip trailing spaces from a field. How can I achieve this?

I've tried using SET ANSI_PADDING ON/OFF within the script, but the trailing spaces still appear.

A: If you're using a select statement to get the data, try:

```
Select rtrim (my_column_name), etc. etc.
```

Question 49: Query Problem

I have a table of results that track each time a student takes a test and the score on the test (must score 100%).

There will be multiple tests and multiple times a test was taken. If they take the same test 3 times there will be three records. I want to query that through this:

```
SELECT TestID, MAX (TryNumber), Score

    FROM tbl_TrackIt

    GROUP BY TestID
```

Since you would need the s core to be part of the GROUP BY this code will not work. How do I get the score for a testid and trynumber in one SQL statement?

A: You can try this:

```
SELECT tbl_TrackIt.TestID, tbl_TrackIt.TryNumber,
tbl_TrackIt.Score

    FROM tbl_TrackIt

    INNER JOIN (SELECT TestID, MAX(TryNumber) AS
tryNum

                    FROM tbl_TrackIt

                    GROUP BY TestID) Tbl1

    ON tbl_TrackIt.TestId = Tbl1.TestId AND

        tbl_TrackIt.TryNumber = Tbl1.tryNum
```

Question 50: International Characters

I have a table with some mixed content stored in nvarchar.
Among the content are Chinese and Russian characters. I have a
textbox in an ASP.NET web form. When I enter and search for
any Chinese or Russian text I do not get any results. How can I
fix this?

A: Try this:

```
SELECT * WHERE WORD LIKE N'%international character%'
```

Question 51: Consolidating Statements

How would I consolidate these three statements? The only
difference is one of the fields in the WHERE statements. I'm
using SQL Server 2005.

CODE:

```
SELECT Inventory.*, Products.IjoistTypeID

FROM Products INNER JOIN Inventory ON
Products.ProductID =

Inventory.ProductID

WHERE (((Inventory.PurchaseOrderID)=" & al_MasterID &
") AND

((Products.LumberTypeID)=3))
```

CODE:

```
SELECT Inventory.*, Products.IjoistTypeID

FROM Products INNER JOIN Inventory ON
Products.ProductID =

Inventory.ProductID

WHERE (((Inventory.ProductionID)=" & al_MasterID & ")
AND
```

```
((Products.LumberTypeID)=3))
```

CODE:

```
SELECT Inventory.*, Products.IjoistTypeID

FROM Products INNER JOIN Inventory ON
Products.ProductID =

Inventory.ProductID

WHERE (((Inventory.ReturnID)=" & al_MasterID & ") AND

((Products.LumberTypeID)=3))
```

A: Try this:

```
SELECT Inventory.*, Products.IjoistTypeID

FROM Products INNER JOIN Inventory ON
Products.ProductID =

Inventory.ProductID

WHERE (Inventory.PurchaseOrderID = al_MasterID  OR

       Inventory.ProductionID   = al_MasterID  OR

       Inventory.ReturnID       = al_MasterID) AND

       (Products.LumberTypeID)=3)
```

Question 52: Grouping by Date with a Date Time Data Type

How do I Group By with date only with a DateTime Data Type? I tried this:

```
SELECT Count (*) as GrossSubmits, SignupDate

FROM dbo.Leads where SignupDate BETWEEN '01-AUG-06'
AND '14-AUG-06'

Group By SignupDate
```

The result is that this breaks out each time as a different grouping. I just want all the records for each date to show as one group. Can this date range bring back Aug 1 through Aug 13 and any date from Aug 14 that are timestamped midnight?

A: This... DateAdd(day, DateDiff(Day, 0, getdate()), 0) will remove the time from a datetime value.

```
SELECT Count(*) as GrossSubmits,

        DateAdd(day, DateDiff(Day, 0, SignupDate), 0)
As SignupDate

FROM  dbo.Leads

where SignupDate BETWEEN '01-AUG-06' AND '14-AUG-06'

Group By DateAdd(day, DateDiff(Day, 0, SignupDate),
0)
```

You do realize that since there is a time component, no records will be returned for 14-AUG-06 unless the time is at midnight.

For your second question, the answer is yes, because of the time component. It's time to mention the 'best practice' method for bringing back dates. If you do this wrong, SQL Server won't be able to use an index if it exists on the date column.

Indexes allow you to retrieve data faster, so obviously you would want to write your queries in a way that allows the indexes to be used.

For example, you could use the 'trick' I showed earlier for stripping the time from the field for use within the where clause.

Where DateAdd(day, DateDiff(Day, 0, SignupDate), 0) between '01-AUG-06' and '14-AUG-06'

This is the BAD way because it will likely cause a table scan and your performance will suffer.

The better way is as follows:

```
Where SignupDate >= '01-AUG-06'

     And SignupDate < '15-AUG-06'
```

Notice that we bumped the 'end date' by 1 day but used LESS THAN, so that any records with 15-AUG-06 will NOT be returned, but all records on the 14th will. Assuming you have an index on the SignupDate field, this last query will use it.

Also notice that we no longer use the "between operator" because the end date must be the 15th, but you don't want records that occur on the 15th at midnight.

Question 53: Sorting a Query Based on a Column's Value

Is it possible if I have a table, Employees, with columns LastName, FirstName, and StartDate, to output all columns with LastName = 'Smith', then all the rest of the columns in alphabetical order?

I'd like one output set that would equal this below:

```
Select LastName,FirstName,StartDate from Employees
where LastName='Smith' order by StartDate desc

Select LastName,FirstName,StartDate from Employees
where LastName != 'Smith' order by StartDate desc
```

I've tried the union operator, but can't use the ORDER BY clause more than once, and just putting it at the end mixes up the results.

A: Do the following:

```
Select
LastName,FirstName,StartDate,TargetName=(difference(L
astName

,'Smith')/4)

from Employees

order by TargetName desc,LastName
```

The different function returns a pattern match of 0-4, four being an exact match. Divide the result by four so any result less than one rounds down to zero will give you a match/no match situation. You can then order it by whether you have a match or not. Check both solutions to see which is faster and then use it.

Question 54: Update Query for Missing Entries in Table

I have a table that stores each record with the primary and foreign keys (i.e., "accid", "prikey"), a system generated date and two generic fields called "task" and "data". Only one of which can be accessed by users.

This table is used for data entry on inspections through a program interface, so the task field can have entries such as "Test Date", "Restest date" "Inspector", and "Test Result". The "data" field has the actual value of that task, such as "6/7/06", "6/7/07", "John Smith", "Fail".

The problem is that some of these fields were imported from another database and only one or two of these "tasks" were identified for a particular inspection (primary key's) record. I need to fill in the missing information based on the missing "tasks".

For example: The table might have a record for "Task"="Retest date" but be missing the "Test Date" for the "Task" record. So I need to update the table and set the "Task" to "Test Date" and update the "data" field where "Task"="Test Date" by the "Restest Date" "data" - 365.

How should I go about this?

A: Do it step-by-step until all is complete. Devise a query to identify the row such as "Task"="Test Date" which corresponds to a particular "Task"="Retest date" row. This query identifies which data is complete.

```
SELECT a.thing_id

FROM Tasks a

JOIN Tasks b ON a.thing_id = b.thing_id

        AND b.task = "Test Date"

WHERE a.task = "Retest date"
```

Here the column thing_id is the key which represents the entity that has the set of tasks. It would be a foreign key in the Tasks tables, referring to whatever is being inspected. You can use that query as a subquery in a NOT IN condition of an outer query.

The outer query SELECTS the values which need to be added to make the table complete.

```
SELECT "Test Date", c.thing_id, DATEADD(day, -365,
c.Data)

FROM Tasks c

WHERE c.thing_id NOT IN (

SELECT a.thing_id

FROM Tasks a
JOIN Tasks b ON a.thing_id = b.thing_id

AND b.task = "Test Date"

WHERE a.task = "Retest date"

)

AND c.Task = "Retest date"
```

Make sure this query gives exactly the one row needed for only the missing rows. Then INSERT the missing rows.

```
INSERT Tasks (task, thing_id, data)

SELECT "Test Date", c.thing_id, DATEADD(day, -365,
c.Data)

FROM Tasks c

WHERE c.thing_id NOT IN (

SELECT a.thing_id

FROM Tasks a

JOIN Tasks b ON a.thing_id = b.thing_id
```

```
AND b.task = "Test Date"

WHERE a.task = "Retest date"

)

AND c.Task = "Retest date"
```

This process will be repeated for each missing task. Make a copy of the table before you do anything. These steps cannot be reversed and the whole procedure is susceptible to mistakes. Sometimes you have to start over because you inserted two -for-one or X when you meant Y.

Question 55: Importing Dates

I'm importing log files from a tab delimited text file (DTS, but this is more of a field type issue). The first field is a date and has recently changed from YYYY-MM-DD to YYYY-DD-MM when importing.

1. Nobody has changed the table or package in yonks.

2. I have checked files pre and post the issue and they have not changed format.

3. The server may have had (non-SQL) patches applied at the weekend.

What else might change the date so that the month and day are swapped in the format?

A: It may be easier to use the SET DATEFORMAT command. If you want yyyy-mm-dd, then you would use:

```
SET DATEFORMAT YMD
```

Put this at the beginning of the query that imports the data. The date format depends upon the SQL Server language setting for the user logged in. It's best to use the ISO unseperated format for dates: YYYYMMDD. Notice that there are no dashes o r slashes to seperate the parts. This type of date will always be interpreted correctly by SQL Server.

Question 56: SQL Server 2005

Is it possible to backup an SQL Server 2000 database and restore it to a SQL Server 2005 Express or to MSDE? Is there a reason I should try to install more than one of these systems on my laptop at the same time?

A: You can safely install SQL Server 2000 and SQL 2005 on the same computer. In fact, under the right circumstances it is recommended.

If you only install SQL express and you attach a n SQL 2000 database to it, then it will automatically be upgraded to the SQL 2005 format. There's no going back. There is no way to later attach that 2005 database to a 2000 instance without recreating the database end exporting the data.

It's better to avoid that if possible. At some time, you may want to send a database back to a customer. If that customer has 2000 and you've attached it to 2005, then you will have a problem sending the database back.

Question 57: Create a Role-Based ER Diagram

I am using SQL Server 2000. I need to create a role-based ER diagram for a new application we're developing. Basically the diagram should have roles, privileges, permissions, etc. of what a user can and cannot see in the application. Where can I see a sample role-based access diagram?

A: You will need to develop this on your own based upon the unique requirements of your application. However, most role-based systems have the following tables set up:

users - stores user account info

users_roles - join table so that multiple users can have the same role, and one

user can have multiple roles

roles - stores the role(s) that are linked to the user accounts

roles_permissions - join table to facilitate many-to-many joins between roles and permissions

permissions - stores the name of the permission, with an appropriate flag value. This can be true/false most of the time.

To determine what is visible in the application, you then need to write functions that will see if a certain permission is connected to the current user, and then display, or not, the sensitive information.

Question 58: Microsoft SQL Server and Oracle Database Server

What are the major differences in query writing and customization using stored procedures etc between Oracle and MS SQL server?

A: The queries are about the same but the functions are screwy like conversions, substrings, dates, and date formatting.

In Oracle, a select statement using IN will parse the query to use indexing where it exists, but SQLServer does full table scans and ignores the indexes.

Using UNION in SQLServer for every component of the IN clause performs the same as Oracle.

Try splitting the query into two statements. Select the IDs from the inner statement into a temporary table, then use it as part of the join in the main SELECT.

Question 59: SQL Statement

I would like to have all the elements belong to this record:

```
= 'Geo' but not the element = 'USA;
```

This is my query:

```
=================
select distinct record.element as element

from record where record.Type =  'Geo'

except

(select record.element as element

from  record

where  record.element = 'USA');
```

A: Try this:

```
select distinct record.element as element

from record

where record.Type =  'Geo'

and record.element <> 'USA'
```

Question 60: Deleting a Column from Table

I add a column to a table by using ALTER table command. How can I remove the column since it does not contain any data?

A: Use the SELECT INTO command to select only the column you want from the source table INTO the new table. You can even reorganize the sequence of the columns this way. After, drop the source table and sp_rename the new table or do another SELECT INTO the original name from that new table.

You can also use this way to insert a new column "in between" existing column, like:

```
SELECT Ca, Cb, Cc, "MyNewCol"=convert (varchar (20)),
Cd INTO MyNEWTable
FROM MyCURRENTTable
```

Question 61: Adding a Quantity

I have a view that I'm setting up. The query works but I would like to add a q uantity that is rolled and subtracted out per line.

For example, I have item 11081 with a qty of 100, and I have two orders that ask for that item. One is asking for a quantity of 70 and the other asking for a qty of 40. I would be short -10 totals for the order. I would like that -10 to show up in the on hand column.

Right now what it will show is 100 - 70 resulting 30 next line 100 -40 resulting 60. The result set looks like this thus far:

```
Select A.OrderNumber, A.PONumber, A.OrderStatus,

REPLACE (A.CustomerNumber, 'WALBENO', 'WAL*MART') AS
CustomerNumber,

A.ShipToName,

                REPLACE (A.WarehouseID, 'B03',
'BEL') AS WarehouseID,
```

83

```
B.ItemNumber, B.QtyOrdered, B.LineType,
A.PromiseDate, sum (C.ItemQuantity)

[On-Hand], (sum (C.ItemQuantity) - QtyOrdered)
QtyResult

FROM dbo.tblOrderMasterfile A INNER JOIN


TranMaster.dbo.tblSalesOrderDetail B ON A.OrderNumber
=

B.OrderNumber

Inner Join PWMS..tblPalletInventory C

ON

B.ItemNumber = C.ItemNumber

Where (A.WarehouseID = 'U105') AND (A.OrderStatus =
'IN PROCESS' OR

                    A.OrderStatus = 'NEW') AND
C.WhseCode = '002'

group by A.PromiseDate, A.OrderNumber, A.PONumber,
A.OrderStatus,

A.CustomerNumber, A.ShipToName, A.WarehouseID,

B.ItemNumber, B.QtyOrdered, B.LineType
```

dataset:

```
SO18134     6047168781                  IN PROCESS
00010150    WAL-MART 6047

U105        14500             10   1    2006-08-08
00:00:00.000    132    122

SO18134     6047168781                  IN PROCESS
00010150    WAL-MART 6047

U105        90341             50   1    2006-08-08
00:00:00.000    1890   1840
```

A: What you want will be extremely processor intensive, and will make your system run slowly and may or may not be accurate depending on if your query contains all the possible order records.

What you have to do is add a column for available items to the item table. Initialize the data by subtracting unfilled orders from existing warehouse count of the item. Have the system automatically decrement this count whenever an order for that item is placed. If an order is cancelled before shipping, have a trigger put the amount back into the record.

Then your query simply needs to access the data in this field which is always up-to-date and doesn't require lengthy calculations through individual records to get the answer each time you run the query.

Question 62: Adding SPROC in Database

How do I run a stored procedure for each database? My idea is to run a stored procedure without having to run it for the first in Query Analyzer in SQL Server 2000, and then select from the dropdown list at the top the next database, click "Execute", then select the next name and so on. Is this possible?

A: You can put them in master, but you would need to prefix it with the database name, for example:

```
EXEC master..usp_myproc
```

The sp_ prefix tells SQL Server to look in master ahead of the current database, which is why user SP's shouldn't use it. I'd strongly advise against putting them in master as these stores the SQL Server global system configuration.

If you create shared objects of any type, create a database to store your server wide objects. Set up a database role for accounts that will need to run it and grant appropriate permissions to the role and make the accounts members of this role.

Then, call them with something like this:

```
EXEC sharedobjs..usp_dosomething
```

Create a database and grant permissions for other dbs to access.

1. Make new db "mynewdb"

2. Make new SPROC "usp_mynewSPROC"

3. To run new SPROC: EXEC mynewdb..usp_mynewSPROC

Dumb question, but is the ".." for a default owner?

You need to change the string to: databasename.ownername.usp_spname if you have a non dbo owner, but this introduces other issues into the equation.

Question 63: Returning Last Dated Row for a Primary Key

I have the trabsactions below:

ID	transDATE	PolicyNum	TransType
1	01/01/2005	abc1	NB
2	01/05/2005	abc1	MTA
3	01/01/2006	abc1	Ren
4	01/04/2006	abc1	MTA
5	01/07/2006	CCC1	NB

I want to return the last NB or REN (by transDATE) for policy number abc1. How can I do it?

A: Try this:

```
select ID

        , transDATE

        , PolicyNum

        , TransType
```

```
    from daTable as T

  where PolicyNum = 'abc'

    and TransType in ( 'NB','REN' )

    and transDATE

      = ( select max(transDATE)

            from datable

          where PolicyNum = T.PolicyNum

            and TransType in ( 'NB','REN' ) )
```

Question 64: Setting Foreign Keys

I am trying to set foreign keys for various tables, and want to make sure I am doing it correctly. I had no problem setting the primary key in the enterprise manager, but I was a little confused setting the foreign key for my child table.

I created my child table and selected the advanced button. Then, I went to the "referenced table" combo and selected my parent table for the reference.

I selected the field I want to name for a foreign key in the "foreign key columns" box. Once I did that, I selected ADD. Once I did that, the top box, labeled "foreign key" was filled in with FK__ 3 ____ 10.

However, when I closed the table and re-opened it again, the values I selected in the foreign key tab to create my foreign key were no longer there. Where did I go wrong?

A: To see if you successfully created your foreign key, type this into an iSQL window:

```
Select * from sysobjects where type='F'
```

Type = 'F' is a foreign key flag. You should see your key name. Or alternately, try to break your foreign key relation.

You can also trycreating an ODBC connection to your SQL server database and working with the database in Interdev. Using the Visual Data Tools is easy. You will be able to create database diagrams once you get there.

Drag and drop fields to create the relations, and indexed the appropriate keys.

Question 65: Column Name and Its Value in the Result Set

Is there a way I can combine the column name and its value in the result set?

For example:

Sample data:

```
AccID   Name    Age
-----   ------  ----
111     Andy    25
```

```
Desired Result:
------------------------
AccID = 111
Name = Andy
Age = 25
```

A: I'll use the column names from your example.

```
Select a.DesiredResult From

(

Select AccID, DesiredResult="AccID = " + str(AccID)
From MyTbl

Union

Select AccID, "Name = " + Name From MyTbl
```

```
Union

Select AccID, "Age = " + str(Age) From MyTbl

) AS a
```

1. Inside the parentheses I have created a union query. Each select statement in the union query selects the unique key column and one of the data columns you want to reformat. The key column is important because it will keep all the rows with the same unique key together. In this example, I assume AccID is a unique key.

2. The second column of the inner query is named "DesiredResult" on the first Select statement of the union query. Note that the following Select statements in the union query do not require a column name.

3. The "AS a" clause at the end of the union query aliases the inner query as "a" for reference by the outer query. This clause must exist and be outside of the trailing parenthesis.

4. "Select a.DesiredResult From" is the outer query that selects the second column from the union or inner query.

5. SQL will not concatenate strings with numbers so I assumed that AccID and Age were numeric and used the str function to convert those columns to strings in order to concatenate to the column name.

6. In my testing, the results were ordered in sequence of the key column and the second column. In this case, the three rows of data per set will be in AccID, Age, Name order not AccID, Name, Age as in the query.

Question 66: Creating Basic Fact Tables

I am trying to create a basic fact table (been on the MS2074 course), and have a dataset to play around with. But I need to transform the table to suit my needs. I need help with what I believe to be an If statement. If my data looks like:

```
Source      Amount
EA          100.00
EA          129.00
Act         220.00
EA           50.00
EA           12.00
Act          23.00
Sect         22.00
Sect         12.00
EA          400.00
Sect        440.00
Act         387.00
```

The source field must become a numeric key.
In Crystal (business objects) syntax one could use a simple:

```
if {source} = 'EA' then 1 else

if {source} = 'Sect' then 2 else

if {source} = 'Act' then 3
```

What is similar syntax in TSQL? I have looked at the IF Statement in Books online, but cannot get it to work.

A: You can try the following:

```
Case Source When  'EA' Then 1

            When 'Sect' Then 2

            When 'Act' Then 3

            Else -1 [green]-- Best practice to have
an else
            End
```

You would be better off creating another table that has source as 1 column and value as another. Then you could simply join the 2 tables to get your desired output.

Question 67: Circumventing the Transaction Log Bottleneck

We are performing a migration from BTrieve to SQL 7. Last night while inserting the results of a two table join that resulted in a table of 14.6 million records, we found that increasing the size of the tempdb, while allowing automatic growth of the log file, with "Truncate on Checkpoint" set to on, was the only way to get this operation to finish.

Is there a way to perform a DML statement such as an insert or an update, but to limit it to 1 million records at a time? I want to perform the same query or procedure but in smaller chunks. Because the incoming data is so twitchy, I do not want to break the query up into parts, because I think in this case, the whole will not equal the sum of the parts.

So if I use the SET ROWCOUNT = 1000000 statement, will my process stop after the first million, or will it continue in increments of a million? I understand that this might have to be programmatically induced.

A: I'm not sure about your process, but SQL Server allows you to limit the number of records processed in a transaction by setting the ROWCOUNT.

```
Set ROWCOUNT 1000000
```

Use Set ROWCOUNT 0 to allow processing of an unlimited number of records. As a quick test, try setting the Recovery Interval to something like 200 and see if that makes a difference.

Just try to optimize this so that it would not take an hour to complete. Tweak the recovery interval, as suggested by foxdev, but I believe the SET ROWCOUNT option is not a valid solution, because processing stops upon reaching the rowcount limit.

SQL Interviews

Question 68: Query List Table with Range to Return State

I have 2 tables. One contains a zip code. The other contains a list of states with minimum to maximum zip codes associated to them. How can I use this list table to return the proper state?

The example below should retrun MA for record 1 and MA for record 2 also...Notice MA has 2 different ranges.

```
Table1:
CBBoats      279E.somethingdrive      5503
GFInc.           20NE.noplaceRd.              1005

Table2:
MA     1001      2791
RI        2801      2940
NH     3031      3897
ME     3901      4992
VT      5001      5495
MA     5501      5544
VT      5601      5907
CT      6001      6389
NY     6390      6390
CT      6401      6928
NJ      7001      8989
NY    10001    14975
PA    15001    19640
```

A: Try the following below:

```
Select *

From    Table1

        Left Join Table2

            On Table1.ZipCode between Table2.MinZip and
Table2.MaxZip
```

Question 69: Sytnax for Openrowset

Does anyone know the syntax for an Openrowset trying to query an Excel Spreadsheet? I am using SQL 2000.

A: Here it is:

```
SELECT * FROM OPENROWSET( 'Microsoft.Jet.OLEDB.4.0',

'Excel 8.0;Database=C:\testing.xls','SELECT * FROM
[Sheet1$]')
```

Question 70: Retrieving Records 'N'

I've got a table with a datetime field, and I want to create a Stored Procedure that retrieves records 'n' days back using an input parameter. This is what I have:

```
input parameter: @tiPastDays INT

declare @dPastDate

@dPastDate = CURRENT_DATE - @tiPastDays

select * from MyTable where tTheDateFieldToAnalyze >=
@dPastDate
```

I want to deal with dates only and don't care about the time portion. How do I segregate unwanted functions?

A: Do the following:

```
declare @tiPastDays int

select @tiPastDays =5

declare @dPastDate datetime

select @dPastDate = convert(varchar(10),dateadd(d, -
@tiPastDays,getdate()),112)

--select @dPastDate
```

```
select * from MyTable where tTheDateFieldToAnalyze >=
@dPastDate
```

Question 71: Trim the Last "," of a String

I have a String with this format: 1, 2, 3, etc. Its size varies, so it could be 1, 2, or 1, 2, 3, 4, 5,

The String always ends with "," and I would like to trim the last ",". How can I do it using SQL Functions?

A: Try the following:

```
declare @test varchar(200)

set @test = '1,2,3,4,5,'

SELECT CASE WHEN RIGHT (@test, 1) = ',' THEN LEFT
(@Test, LEN (@test)-1) ELSE @test END
```

Question 72: Retrieving Two Records Per ID

I have thousands of records with one or more records per project ID. I want to only retrieve two records per id based on the two most recent timestamps or one record if there is only one.

```
Id        timestamp

1         2006-07-09 13:00:00
1         2006-07-01 09:30:00
2         2006-07-03 10:15:00
2         2006-06-30 12:18:00
3         2006-06-18 04:00:00
3         2006-06-01 08:13:00
4         2006-07-25 14:35:00
4         2006-07-24 12:35:00
```

How do I accomplish the following?

A: Do the following:

```
Select A.ID, A.timestamp

from mytable A

WHERE A.timestamp in

    (

        Select Top 2 timestamp from

        mytable B where A.ID=B.ID

        Order by timestamp DESC

    )
```

Question 73: Create a Folder and Copy a File

I need to create a job in SQL 2000 that will copy a specified file in a specified directory. If that directory doesn't exist then how should I create it? Is this possible in SQL?

A: You will have to use an ActiveX programming in a DTS that uses File system object:

```
Dim objFSO, objFile, objFolder

Set objFSO =
CreateObject("Scripting.FileSystemObject")

Set objFolder =
objFSO.GetFolder("D:\Data\LOG\SendLog\")
...

For Each objFile in objFolder.Files
...

objFile.move "D:\Data\LOG\SendLog\Test\"
```

Question 74: Calculations on Row Data

I want to run a query to subtract col_2 from col_1 and put the difference in col_3. Col_2 and col_1 already have values in them. Can this be done in a single query statement?

A: To update the table, do the following:

```
Update Table

Set    Col3 = Col1-Col2

To return the data...

Select Col1 - Col2 As Col3

From   Table
```

Question 75: Reading ata from Registry

We are trying to use the pr_checkport stored procedure to check the port that the current SQL Server instance is using and if it is on the wrong port, it will page us. The read from the registry worked for SQL Serve 2000, but with 2005 the location of SQL Server changed. It still works if we alter the stored procedure to match the new directory in the Registry, however, when we have an instance of SQL Server 2005 installed over 2000, the location is different due to the extra instance, and for some reason I can't seem to get this to work.

Here is a snippet from the stored procedure, which uses an extended stored procedure called xp_instance_regread to read from the registry. The directory I put below matches our current Test instance directory that holds the port number for the instance, but I get the error printed below:

CODE:

```
declare @SmoDefaultFile nvarchar(512)

exec master.dbo.xp_instance_regread
N'HKEY_LOCAL_MACHINE',

N'Software\Microsoft\Microsoft SQL

Server\SQL2005JESS\MSSQLServer\SuperSocketNetLib\Tcp'
, N'DefaultData',

@SmoDefaultFile OUTPUT
```

CODE:

```
RegOpenKeyEx() returned error 2, 'The system cannot
find the file specified.'

Msg 22001, Level 1, State 1
```

How I can get it to read the port number for the current instance?

A: In SQL 2005 servers this code works for servers that have a static port set.

CODE:

```
declare @SmoDefaultFile nvarchar(512)

exec master.dbo.xp_instance_regread
N'HKEY_LOCAL_MACHINE',

N'Software\Microsoft\MSSQLServer\MSSQLServer\SuperSoc
ketNetLib\Tcp\IPAll\', N'TcpPort',

@SmoDefaultFile OUTPUT

print @SmoDefaultFile
```

For instances which have a dynamic port this code worked.

CODE:

```
declare @SmoDefaultFile nvarchar(512)

exec master.dbo.xp_instance_regread
N'HKEY_LOCAL_MACHINE',

N'Software\Microsoft\MSSQLServer\MSSQLServer\SuperSoc
ketNetLib\Tcp\IPAll\',

N'TcpDynamicPorts',

@SmoDefaultFile OUTPUT

print @SmoDefaultFile
```

That path in the registry doesn't change when you change instances. It stays the same. The function "xp_instance_regread" does the converting to the correct instance specific path for you.

Question 76: Returning the Records

How can I return the records of Table A where those records are
not in Table B? Comparing to inventory tables, one is the master
and the other is the pricing table, items were accidently deleted
from the master. So I need to remove the associated record from
the pricing table. The Item Number is the primary key.

A: Try this:

```
SELECT TableA.*

FROM TableA

LEFT JOIN TableB ON TableA.PK = TableB.FK

WHERE TableB.FK IS NULL
```

Question 77: SQL Server Linked Server Problem

I have a problem with an SQL Server Linked Server and OLE DB.

```
WinNT (SP6)
SQL Server 7 SP3 (7.00.961)
MDAC Version 2.6 RTM
Oracle Client 8.1.7

Oracle DB 8.0.6 (running on a UNIX system)
```

I cannot read any data using the linked server from the Oracle
Tables.

Using Query Analyser ...Example Program......

```
EXEC sp_addlinkedserver 'scs', 'Oracle', 'MSDAORA',
'scs01p' -- TNS Name is 'scs01p'
GO
EXEC sp_addlinkedsrvlogin 'scs', FALSE, NULL,
'digitron', 'digitron'
GO
```

```
SELECT * FROM scs..DIGITRON.NEILTEST1
```

This produces the following error:

```
(1 row(s) affected)
(1 row(s) affected)
Server added.
(1 row(s) affected)
(0 row(s) affected)
(1 row(s) affected)

Server: Msg 7370, Level 16, State 2, Line 1
One or more properties could not be set on the query
for OLE DB provider 'MSDAORA'.  The provider could
not support a required property.
[OLE/DB provider returned message: Multiple-step OLE
DB operation generated errors. Check each OLE DB
status value, if available. No work was done.]
```

Yet, if I execute the following SP from QA:

```
EXEC sp_tables_ex scs
```

I get a full system catalog / owner / table list. So I assume that the Linked Server is all OK. I have also tried using the MS ODBC Driver for Oracle, this produces the same results. I can access the data from the remote Oracle DB using the SQL*PLUS & ODBC Test Tools provided with Oracle.

A: Change the remote query timeout option value in SQL Server from 200 (default) to 0 (0 = Infite wait).

Question 78: To See Output in Query Analyzer

I have a sproc with an output parameter. When I run the sproc in Query Analyzer, all I get is the success message, but the output does not appear. In the Query Aanalyzer I run it like this:

```
Exec dbo.get_available_schedule_credit2 100,5,3
```

(There are input parameters too.) This is the SP. It is not complete for my purposes but it should return the credit limit for counterparty 100:

```
--------------------------
CREATE PROCEDURE [dbo].get_available_schedule_credit2

@counterpartyID int,

@scheduleID int,

@credit_out int output

AS

declare @total_guarantor_commits int

declare @leg_amounts int

declare @initial_credit int

select @credit_out =0

select @initial_credit=CreditLimit from
tblCounterparties where

tblCounterparties.CounterpartyID = @counterpartyID

select @credit_out = @credit_out + @initial_credit

Return
GO
--------------------------
```

As a test I put this in Q.A.:

```
Select CreditLimit from tblCounterparties where
tblCounterparties.CounterpartyID = 100;
```

I got back the credit limit. But how do you structure the syntax in Q.A. with the sp to get a value back while in Q.A.?

A: Try this:

```
DECLARE @credit_out integer

SET @credit_out = 3

Exec dbo.get_available_schedule_credit2
100,5,@credit_out OUTPUT
print @credit_out
```

You need to pass in a variable with the "output" keyword containing your input value, for example:

```
Declare @credit int

select @credit = 3

Exec dbo.get_available_schedule_credit2 100,5,@credit
output

select 'credit is ' + (cast @credit as varchar (5))
```

Your output value then goes into the same variable name which you can reference later on in your code.

Question 79: Selecting a Recordset

I have a very large table that is basically structured like this:

Category	Score	Type
1	90	0
2	3	0
2	87	1
3	65	0

Notice that Category 2 has two records (of type 0 and 1). What I need to do is select a recordset that excludes all 0-type records where its category also has a 1-type.
So the result would be:

Category	Score	Type
1	90	0
2	87	1
3	65	0

Note that the Score of the 1-type might not always be larger than the equivalent 0-type. I thought of just grouping on Category using the MAX aggregate function, but that won't always work for score. I need the actual score assigned to the MAX Type (the type of 1). How do I accomplish this?

A: Try this:

```
Select  Table.Category,

        Table.Type,

        Table.Score

From    Table

        Inner Join

          (

          Select Category,

                 Max(Type) As Type

          From    Table
```

```
) As A

On   Table.Category = A.Category

And Table.Type = A.Type
```

Question 80: Building a Case Statement

I have the following part of a select statement that I need to break down further.

```
,Cost =

CASE Summary.CreditOrDebit WHEN 'C' THEN
GLCode.Cost*-1    ELSE GLCode.Cost END

Now I need to say if Cost is <= 0 then "Range 0"

 if Cost is > 0 and < 500 then "Range 1"

 if Cost is >=500 and < 1000 then "Range 2"
```

I don't think I Can use 'Cost' but I need to test it to see if the transaction is a credit/debit, and then change the sign if needed to do my comparison.

```
,Range =

  CASE WHEN Summary.CreditOrDebit = 'C' then "RANGE
0"

       ELSE

    WHEN GLCode.Cost > 0 and GLCode.Cost <= 500 then
```

Is there any other way I can approach this?

A: CreditOrDebit = 'C' if cost is positive and 'D' if cost is negative.

```
Range = Case When Abs(GLCode.Cost) Between 0 And 500

                Then 'Range 0'
```

```
        When Abs(GLCode.Cost) Between 501 And
1000

            Then 'Range 1'

        When Abs(GLCode.Cost) Between 1001 And
1000

            Then 'Range 2'

        Else 'Some other range'

        End
```

Question 81: Case Statement in a View

I have written a view with a case statement which returns records that doesn't work.

```
SELECT      TempID, DateEntered, CountEntered,
DateResolved, CountResolved, CASE

DateEntered WHEN isnull (DateEntered, 1)

                THEN DateResolved ELSE
DateEntered END AS TheDate

FROM        TempDailyReport

ORDER BY DateEntered, DateResolved
```

I wanted TheDate column to be equal to DateResolved when there was no value found in DateEntered. It leaves it blank every time. A sample of the data returned is below:

```
TempID DateEntered CountEntered DateResolved
CountResolved TheDate
153         BLANK               BLANK
1/2/2005            1                       BLANK
154         BLANK               BLANK
1/26/2006           1                       BLANK
155         BLANK               BLANK
2/14/2006           1                       BLANK
1           1/2/2006            10
1/2/2006            8                       1/2/2006
```

2	1/3/2006	8	
1/3/2006		8	1/3/2006

How do I fix this?

A: Try this:

```
SELECT     TempID, DateEntered, CountEntered,
DateResolved, CountResolved,

COALESCE (DateEntered, DateResolved) AS TheDate

FROM       TempDailyReport

ORDER BY DateEntered, DateResolved
```

Question 82: SQL Statement Dilemma

I've created an SQL that pulls all ORDER_NAME that have a O_PROMPT associated with it. Here it is:

```
select i.PERF_FAC_ID, i.PERF_DEPT_ID,  i.ORDER_NAME,
q.PROMPT_TEXT, q.MAND_FL,

r.VALUE_TEXT from O_ITEM i, O_ITEM_PROMPT p, O_PROMPT
q, O_PROMPT_LOV r

where i.ORDER_ITEM_SEQ = p.ORDER_ITEM_SEQ

and p.PROMPT_SEQ = q.PROMPT_SEQ

and r.PROMPT_SEQ = p.PROMPT_SEQ

and p.PROMPT_SEQ > 60

and i.PERF_FAC_ID = 'PP'

order by i.PERF_DEPT_ID
```

How do I include those ORDER_NAME that have no O_PROMPT associated with it? I'm using some a freeware called DbVisualizer to write this.

A: LEFT OUTER JOIN is exactly what you need.

```
select i.PERF_FAC_ID
, i.PERF_DEPT_ID
, i.ORDER_NAME
, q.PROMPT_TEXT
, q.MAND_FL
, r.VALUE_TEXT
from O_ITEM i
left outer
join O_ITEM_PROMPT p
on p.ORDER_ITEM_SEQ = i.ORDER_ITEM_SEQ
and p.PROMPT_SEQ > 60
left outer
join O_PROMPT q
on q.PROMPT_SEQ = p.PROMPT_SEQ
left outer
join O_PROMPT_LOV r
on r.PROMPT_SEQ = p.PROMPT_SEQ
where i.PERF_FAC_ID = 'PP'
order
by i.PERF_DEPT_ID
```

Question 83: Move a Database to Another Server

Is it possible to have a database on a test server and move it to another? How can this be done?

A: It is possible. Just follow these steps:

1. Make a full backup of y our database.

2. Create a new database "YourDatabase" on your test server.

3. Restore the backup to this database and check 'Force restore over existing database' on the Options-tab.

4. When the folders with the MDF/LDF files are different on both machines you also must change the path in the 'Restore database as' fields.

You have to use the sp_attach_db. Detaching the database and copying the data file and log file will work great. The only thing to be wary about is whether you are using SQL 7 or SQL 2000. Using the sp_attach_db procedure is a snap, but in SQL 7 the servers have to have the same sort order and unicode collation settings. If you selected the default install on both machines for SQL7 , then this is a breeze.

Question 84: Grouping by SP with a Text Field

How can I do a group by SP with a TEXT Field? I am trying to select the group by info and then join it to another table to get the TEXT info. This is what I have so far:

```
ALTER PROCEDURE dbo.spSalesByDateWithReferer

(@FromDate smalldatetime,

@ToDate smalldatetime)

AS

SELECT      Referer

FROM        dbo.tContacts as ST, (

SELECT      MIN (dbo.tContacts.Surname) AS Surname,
SUM (dbo.tSaleDetails.PlotPrice) AS

Volume, dbo.tSale.ContactID

FROM          dbo.tSale INNER JOIN

dbo.tContacts ON dbo.tSale.ContactID =
dbo.tContacts.ContactID INNER JOIN

dbo.tSaleDetails ON dbo.tSale.SaleID =
dbo.tSaleDetails.SaleID

WHERE      (dbo.tSale.DateSold BETWEEN CONVERT
(DATETIME, @FromDate, 102) AND

CONVERT (DATETIME, @ToDate, 102))

GROUP BY dbo.tSale.ContactID AS SA

WHERE ST.ContactID= SA.ContactID
```

The referer is the TEXT field which is in Contacts.

A: This inner part of the select is working properly:

```
SELECT MIN (dbo.tContacts.Surname) AS Surname,
```

```
SUM (dbo.tSaleDetails.PlotPrice) AS Volume,

dbo.tSale.ContactID

FROM    dbo.tSale

INNER JOIN dbo.tContacts

ON dbo.tSale.ContactID = dbo.tContacts.ContactID

INNER JOIN dbo.tSaleDetails

ON dbo.tSale.SaleID = dbo.tSaleDetails.SaleID
WHERE (dbo.tSale.DateSold BETWEEN CONVERT (DATETIME,
@FromDate, 102) AND

CONVERT (DATETIME, @ToDate, 102)
```

To add more to it, you need to make this a sub-query, with an alias, and return the fields:

```
ALTER PROCEDURE dbo.spSalesByDateWithReferer
(@FromDate smalldatetime,

@ToDate smalldatetime)

AS

SELECT Referer

FROM    dbo.tContacts As ST

Inner Join (

SELECT MIN (dbo.tContacts.Surname) AS Surname,

SUM (dbo.tSaleDetails.PlotPrice) AS Volume,

dbo.tSale.ContactID

FROM    dbo.tSale

INNER JOIN dbo.tContacts

ON dbo.tSale.ContactID = dbo.tContacts.ContactID

INNER JOIN dbo.tSaleDetails
```

```
ON dbo.tSale.SaleID = dbo.tSaleDetails.SaleID

WHERE (dbo.tSale.DateSold BETWEEN CONVERT (DATETIME,
@FromDate, 102) AND

CONVERT (DATETIME, @ToDate, 102)

GROUP BY dbo.tSale.ContactId

) As SA

On ST.ContactId = SA.ContactId
```

Why don't you modify your input parameters to accept DateTime and then skip the convert instead of converting SmallDateTime to DateTime? This assumes that DateSold is a DateTime field. Generally, you are better off NOT converting datatype when possible to improve performance.

Question 85: Converting Number/Text to Date

I am running SQL Server 2000. I have a field which comes in as a string of numbers representing a date. For example:

122506 = christmas of 2006.

70406 = the 4th of July.

I need to get this information stored in a DateTime field in the database. I have tried storing the number as both a bigint and a char with equal failure. How do I accomplish this?

A: Try this:

```
Declare @Temp VarChar(20)

Set @Temp = '70406'

select Convert(DateTime, right(@Temp, 2) +
Left(Right('000000' + @Temp, 6), 4))
```

It appears that any date prior to Oct 1, will be represented by a 7 character string (because the month number can be represented with a single digit). So we need to first format the number to a standard 6 digits. Right ('000000' + @Temp, 6) will add a leading 0 if need be. So 70406 will become 070406.

Taking the 2 right characters of this string will get the year. Taking the left 4 characters of the padded string will return the month and day (in that order). So, just before converting to DateTime data type, 70406 becomes 060704. SQL Serv er's convert function will correctly interpret this as YYMMDD.

Question 86: Dynamic SQL Statement

I'm trying to build a dynamic SQL statement and put it into my stored procedure, but I'm getting an error and can't figure out what's wrong. Below is code section and assigment part will be replaced with actual values from selections once I put it into sproc.

```
declare

@ProjectAreaKey int,

@MaterialTypeID varchar(10),

@BaseMaterial bit,

@UserID varchar(10),

@LevelCost decimal(15,3) ,

@LevelMargin int,

@LevelCostColumnName varchar(50),

@LevelMarginColumnName varchar(50),

@SQL varchar(3000)

set @LevelCostColumnName = 'LevelCost'

set @LevelMarginColumnName = 'LevelMargin'
```

```
set @ProjectAreaKey = 1

set @MaterialTypeID = 'Carpet'

set @LevelMargin = 3

set @LevelCost = 14

set @BaseMaterial = 1

set @UserID = 'Gosha'

set @SQL = 'insert into CostCalculationWrk
(ProjectAreaKey,MatlTypeID,BaseMaterial,UserID,'

        + @LevelCostColumnName + ',' +
@LevelMarginColumnName + ') '

        + ' values (' + @ProjectAreaKey + ',''' +
@MaterialTypeID + ''','

        + @BaseMaterial + ',''' + @UserID + ''','

        + @LevelCost + ',' + @LevelMargin + ')'
```

I also get the syntax error:

```
Conversion failed when converting the varchar value
'insert into CostCalculationWrk
(ProjectAreaKey,MatlTypeID,BaseMaterial,UserID,LevelC
ost,LevelMargin)  values (' to data type int.
```

How do I fix this?

A: Some of your variables are numbers (bit, numeric, int). You need to convert to varchar while you build the string you will eventually execute.

```
set @SQL = 'insert into CostCalculationWrk
(ProjectAreaKey,MatlTypeID,BaseMaterial,UserID,'

        + @LevelCostColumnName + ',' +
@LevelMarginColumnName + ') '

        + ' values (' + Convert(varchar(20),
@ProjectAreaKey) + ',''' + @MaterialTypeID + ''','
```

```
             + Convert(varchar(20), @BaseMaterial) +
',''' + @UserID + ''','

             + Convert(varchar(20), @LevelCost) + ','
+ Convert(varchar(20), @LevelMargin) + ')'
```

Question 87: Semi-Complex Query Question

I am trying to write one query to give me:

1. The total count of records in the table.

2. The count of records where phone number is null.

Grouped by source code, I want to achieve this without modifying my table or using a view. This is what I have right now:

```
SELECT keycode, PHONEIND = CASE

WHEN PHONE IS NULL THEN '1'

ELSE '0'

END)

FROM tblname

WHERE imp_date > '2006-05-15'
```

What I want to see is count (ID) and sum (PHONEIND) grouped by keycode.

A: Try this:

```
Select KeyCode,

        Count(*) As TotalCount,

        Sum(Case When Phone Is NULL Then 1 Else 0 End)
As CountOfNulls

From     tblName

Where   imp_date > '2006-05-15'

Group By KeyCode
```

Question 88: t'Times and t'SoteVisits

I have two tables named tTimes and tSiteVisits.

tTimes:
```
TimeID
Time
```

tSiteVisits:
```
SiteVisitID
TimeID
SiteVisitDate
SiteID
```

I need to find any available time that have not been used in tSiteVisits. Where I pass parameters:

`@SiteVisitDate and @SiteID`.

This works when I just pass the Date:

```
ALTER PROCEDURE dbo.spSiteVisitTimes
(@SiteVisitDate datetime)
AS SELECT        dbo.tSiteVisitTimes.TimesID,
dbo.tSiteVisitTimes.Times
FROM         dbo.tSiteVisits INNER JOIN
                    dbo.tSiteVisitTimes ON
dbo.tSiteVisits.SiteVisitTimeID <>
dbo.tSiteVisitTimes.TimesID
WHERE        (dbo.tSiteVisits.SiteVisitDate =
CONVERT(DATETIME, @SiteVisitDate, 102))
```

But when I add @SiteID I get nothing. Why is this?

A: Try this:

```
ALTER PROCEDURE dbo.spSiteVisitTimes

(@SiteVisitDate datetime,

@SiteID int)

AS

SELECT TimesID, Times
```

```
FROM dbo.tTimes

WHERE dbo.tTimes.TimesId NOT IN

(SELECT TimeID FROM tSiteVisits

WHERE tSiteVisits.SiteVisitDate = CONVERT (DATETIME,
@SiteVisitDate, 102) AND

SiteID = @SiteId)
```

Question 89: Creating a Table Name

I've got a Stored Procedure and I want to create the table name
dynamically and use it in the procedure. I have the following SP:

```
ALTER PROCEDURE dbo.ASI_SC_GetMenuOptions

    @UserID int,

    @LastProductID int,

    @CustomerCode varchar (10)

  AS

    DECLARE @TableName varchar (50)

    SET @TableName = "SC_" + @CustomerCode +
".UserMenuOptions umo"

    SELECT mo.MenuOptionID, Parent, ItemNumber, Item,
TargetAction, StatusTip

    FROM MenuOptions mo (nolock)

    INNER JOIN @TableName

    ON mo.MenuOptionID=umo.MenuOptionID

    AND umo.UserID=@UserID

    WHERE AllProducts=1 OR mo.MenuOptionID IN

    (SELECT mop.MenuOptionID
```

```
FROM MenuOptionProducts mop

WHERE mop.ProductID=@LastProductID)

ORDER BY Parent, ItemNumber

GO

SET QUOTED_IDENTIFIER OFF

GO

SET ANSI_NULLS ON

GO
```

I want the above to generate the following line for the FROM statement:

```
FROM SC_FAAO.UserMenuOptions umo
```

But I get the following error:

```
Server: Msg 137, Level 15, State 2, Procedure
ASI_SC_GetMenuOptions, Line 34
Must declare the variable '@TableName'.
```

A: It will not work. You need dynamic SQL. Try this:

```
ALTER PROCEDURE dbo.ASI_SC_GetMenuOptions

@UserID int,

@LastProductID int,

@CustomerCode varchar (10)

 AS

Declare @BigSQLString varchar (6666)

DECLARE @TableName varchar (50)

SET @TableName = "SC_" + @CustomerCode +
".UserMenuOptions umo"
```

```
Select @BigSQLString ='SELECT mo.MenuOptionID,
Parent, ItemNumber, Item, TargetAction,

StatusTip

FROM MenuOptions mo (nolock)

INNER JOIN ' + @TableName +

'ON mo.MenuOptionID=umo.MenuOptionID

AND umo.UserID=' + convert (varchar, @UserID) +'

WHERE AllProducts=1 OR mo.MenuOptionID IN

(SELECT mop.MenuOptionID

FROM MenuOptionProducts mop

WHERE mop.ProductID=' + convert (varchar,
@LastProductID) +'

ORDER BY Parent, ItemNumber'

Exec (@BigSQLString)

GO

SET QUOTED_IDENTIFIER OFF

GO

SET ANSI_NULLS ON
GO
```

Question 90: Calculated Column

I have an SQL Select command with a calculated column that has been working for years in an Access database. Now passing this same Select to SQL Server, it does not work.

```
SELECT Invoice.Date,Invoice.Name,Invoice.Total,
```

And this is the calculated column:

```
(Invoice.Paid + Invoice.TotalTax * Abs(Invoice.Paid >
0) * Abs(Invoice.PayType <> 'EFP'))"

Explanation: Invoice.TotalTax allways has some
positive value, but Invoice.TotalTax must be changed
to 0 if Invoice.Paid is 0, or if Invoice.PayType is
'EFP'
```

A: Here's the correct code:

```
(Invoice.Paid + Invoice.TotalTax *

 CASE WHEN Invoice.Paid <= 0 OR Invoice.PayType =
'EFP' THEN 0

      ELSE 1 END)
```

Question 91: DTS Task

I am not familiar with DTS. I have a task that is taking a large text file and automatically imports it into a Sybase table. I suspect that it is using BCP to do so. If it does, I am afraid I will need to write an audit program, as there is no way to make triggers fire with BCP. What should I do next?

A: In the DTS task, check to see if that does the load from the text file and look at the options. If fast load is checked the DTS uses BCP to shove the data in bypassing things like triggers. You can uncheck the box and the trigger will run, but the performance may be unacceptable. You may want to use the fast load option and then fire a stored procedure that sends your emails. I have gone both routes in the past depending on the performance issues.

Question 92: Inserting Spaces

I have the following table - table1:

RecID	RecName	DisplayName
1	CreateDate	NULL
2	CreateUser	NULL
3	ModDate	NULL
4	ModUser	NULL
5	LastName	NULL
6	FirstName	NULL
7	ContactFirstName	NULL

Below is the desired output:

RecID	RecName	DisplayName
1	CreateDate	Create Date
2	CreateUser	Create User
3	ModDate	Mod Date
4	ModUser	Mod User
5	LastName	Last Name
6	FirstName	First Name
7	ContactFirstName	Contact First Name

What is the best way to insert spaces?

A: Create this UDF:

```
Alter Function dbo.AddSpaces

    (

    @Original VarChar (8000)

    )

Returns VarChar (8000)

AS

Begin
```

```
Declare @SingleCharacter VarChar (1)

Declare @i Integer

Declare @Output VarChar (8000)

Set @i = 1

Set @Output = ''

While @i <= Len (@Original)

Begin

Select @SingleCharacter = SubString (@Original, @i,
1)

If ASCII (@SingleCharacter) Between 65 And 90

Begin

Set @Output = @Output + ' '

End

Set @Output = @Output + @SingleCharacter

Set @i = @i + 1

End

Return LTrim (@Output)

End
```

Then:

```
Update TableName Set DisplayName = dbo.AddSpaces
(RecName)
```

Question 93: Creating Date Range

I need to create a q uery that produces a date range. The start date needs to always be Sunday and the next date needs to be Saturday. For example I would like to have a drop down that reads like this:

05/07/2006 - 05/13/2006

05/14/2006 - 05/20/2006

05/21/2006 - 05/27/2006

I want the user that will be able to select the date they like. How can this be done?

A: There are two things you need to do:

Step1: create number table, do this only once. You will use this table always so don't delete it.

CODE:

```
Create out Pivot table ** Do this only once--
populate it with 1000 rows

CREATE TABLE NumberPivot (NumberID INT PRIMARY KEY)

DECLARE @intLoopCounter INT

SELECT @intLoopCounter =0

WHILE @intLoopCounter <=1000

BEGIN

INSERT INTO NumberPivot

VALUES (@intLoopCounter)

SELECT @intLoopCounter = @intLoopCounter +1

END

GO
```

Step 2 : the code to return the rows

CODE:

```
DECLARE @StartDate datetime

Select @StartDate ='05/07/2006'

Declare @RowsToReturn int

Select @RowsToReturn = 50

SELECT DATEADD (wk, numberID, @StartDate), DATEADD
(dd,-1, (DATEADD

(Wk, numberID+1, @StartDate)))

FROM dbo.NumberPivot

WHERE NumberID <= @RowsToReturn

And DATEADD (wk, numberID, @StartDate) >=@StartDate

ORDER BY 1
```

Question 94: Changing Location of Data Files of a Database

I need to change the location of the data files for a database. We are running out of disk space on the c: drive of the SQL Server. My questions are: 1) How is this done? 2) Are there any caveats to this as I have several SSIS packages that are pointing to this particular database?

A: For your first question, you can detach the database, and then copy the .mdf and .ldf files to the new location. Then attach the database pointing to the files in the new location.

For your second question, it should not affect your SSIS packages.

Question 95: Installation Problem

I'm running XP Pro and I can't install SQLServer2000 on my machine. It keeps telling me that the "Microsoft SQL Server Standard Edition server component is not supported on this operating system."

I've installed 2000 on an XP machine before. A colleague suggested that I might have an incompatible version of MDAC. I checked it out and it is 2.8 (from a DB2) installation. Could this be the problem? If so, can I have two versions of MDAC on my machine at the same time?

A: Your problem has nothing to do with the version of MDAC which you have installed.

You can only install MSDE, Personal, Trial, or Developer editions on a non-server OS (Windows 9x, Windows 2000/XP Pro). Standard and Enterprise Edition can on be installed on a Server OS.

Question 96: Convert an INT Field

I have an INT field called date that displays todays date like 20060516. In my where clauses I need to compare this field with the getdate function like this:

```
Select

tblTest.ID

From

tblTest

Where

tblTest.Date = Getdate ()
```

How do I convert this date field (to a datetime field 103) so it will show todays date like 16052006 and then compare it to the getdate function?

A: Do the following:

```
Select

tblTest.ID

From

tblTest

Where

tblTest.Date = convert (int, replace (convert
(varchar, getdate (), 103),'/',''))
```

To test, runs this:

```
select convert (int, replace (convert (varchar,
getdate (), 103),'/',''))
```

Question 97: Reference a Server/Database

I am using the same view for 140 individual tables across multiple copies of the same database. Each have different names on 6 different servers. Is there a way to generically reference a server and/or database name within a view?

Example 1:

```
create view dbo.MyTrans

as

select * from @server.@dbname.dbo.transactions
```

Example 2 :

```
create view dbo.MyTrans

as

select * from @dbname1.dbo.transactions as t

inner join @dbname2.dbo.control as c

on t.appid = c.appid
```

Note: I only use select * as an example; I am using named columns in the actual views.

A: You can't use variables for the object names in a query. Do this and you'll have to use Dyanamic SQL which raises security and performance issues of its own.

```
declare @CMD varchar(1000)

delcare @db sysname

declare @server sysname

set @server = 'SERVER1'

set @db = 'DB3'
```

```
set @CMD = 'select * from ' + @server + '.' + @db +
'.dbo.table'

exec @CMD
```

This would only work in a stored procedure. Views don't accept paramaters.

Question 98: Drop an Existing Table

I want to query if a file exists in the database. I know it's in the 'benchmark' database. I tried doing this:

```
If exists table1 in information_schema.tables
Drop table table1
```

Is there another approach I can use?

A: Try this:

```
If Exists (SELECT * from mydb.dbo.Sysobjects

WHERE xtype='U' and name='table1')

Begin

Drop Table table1

End
```

Question 99: User and Permission Table

How can I transfer the user, permission, and access tables to a new database? For example:

```
database apple --> database apple1
```

I managed to transfer all other user created DB, but I can't transfer the master database.

A: Follow these steps:

1. Right-Click on the "Apple" DB

2. Select "All Tasks"

3. Select "Generate Scripts"

4. Under the "General" Tab, Select all objects

5. Unser the "Formatting" Tab ensure nothing is clicked

6. Under the "Options" Tab,
   Click "Script Database Users and Roles"
   Click "Script Object-Level Permissions"

7. Save this script and run it on your "Apple1" database.

Question 100: Inserting Records from Table Order

How do I insert records from table Order into table OrderCopy based on a given date? I am using the following query, but I keep getting an error that says table order copy already exists in the database. How do I accomplish this?

Here is my query:

```
SELECT *

INTO OrderCopy

FROM Order

WHERE (OrdDate = '5/10/2005')
```

A: If you select into, it will create a table. Your syntax would be:

```
Insert Into OrderCopy (Field1, Field2, etc)

Select Field1, Field2, etc

From    Order

Where (OrdDate = '5/10/2005')
```

Acknowlegements

http://www.tek-tips.com/threadminder.cfm?pid=183

Index